BRISTOL
BLENHEIM

BRISTOL
BLENHEIM

CHAZ BOWYER

LONDON

IAN ALLAN LTD

Dedication

To all Blenheim crews who 'failed to return' —
especially Eric D., a schooldays friend who died in a
Blenheim gun turret, aged 18 years.

Acknowledgements

The author wishes to acknowledge most gratefully
the generous and expert assistance in compilation of
the following (in alphabetical order): Sqn Ldr
R. C. B Ashworth, RAF Retd; P. Bartlett; P. G.
Bowen; E. G. Caban; Sqn Ldr A. F. Carlisle DFC
RAF Retd; F. S. Cooper; M. J. Cuny; D. Gray of
Walkers Studios, Scarborough; P. H. T. Green;
F. C. Hambly of Weybridge-Bristol Division, British
Aerospace; Flt Lt F. Harrison; E. Hine of IWM
Photographic Library; D. E. James; S. W. Lee AFC,
DFM; H. Long; R. W. Mack of RAF Museum,
Hendon; J. Mansell; P. M. C. Morris; K. Munson; B.
Robertson; J. A. H. Shepherd; J. W. R. Taylor; Flt
Lt A. Thomas, RAF; Sqn Ldr D. W. Warne, RAF.

Chaz Bowyer
Norwich, 1983

Contents

First published 1984

ISBN 0 7110 1351 9

Published by Ian Allan Ltd, Shepperton, Surrey;
and printed by Ian Allan Printing Ltd at their works
at Coombelands in Runnymede, England.

Introduction

It would be foolish — or conceited — to claim a single volume as a 'complete' history of any firstline, operational aircraft of World War 2. This book is simply an attempt to give the Bristol Blenheim 'family' a well-overdue niche in the published records of that aerial conflict, albeit in highly condensed form. Like so many outstanding British aircraft designs 'born' in the immediate pre-1939 era — de Havilland's superb Mosquito comes readily to mind in this context — the Blenheim resulted from a private venture design which *then* provoked officialdom's interest. On its introduction in 1937 to RAF squadron use the Blenheim could coolly outpace any contemporary RAF interceptor fighter by a good margin of pure speed; hence the contemporary advertised claim by its manufacturers as the 'fastest bomber in the world'. Over the next seven years or so Blenheims gave wide, varied, and doughty service in almost every possible role and in virtually every theatre of war, bearing the military livery of several nations. The early claims to fame of the Blenheim were quickly outpaced by the rapid evolution of bigger, faster, better-armed bomber designs once World War 2 gathered momentum; yet without the trojan work — and sacrifices — of the Blenheims and their courageous crews in the early war years, the RAF's offensive capability might have been near-impotent.

Below
Neat echelon of Blenheim Is of 114 Squadron, 1938.
K7041, 'K' was fitted with dual controls.
Flight International

1
Roots

The true genesis of the Bristol Blenheim bombers derived from a desire by Frank Barnwell, chief designer and engineer of the Bristol Aeroplane Company, and his team at Filton, to produce a civil commercial light transport aircraft capable of cruising speeds of at least 250mph, a figure well in advance of any contemporary civil counterpart. On 28 July 1933, Barnwell translated his initial thoughts into preliminary sketches for a twin-engined, low-wing monoplane, with enclosed cockpit and cabin to accommodate two pilots and six passengers. For power it was intended to use Bristol Aquila Is; sleeve-valve, air-cooled radials still under development by the company's engineers under the aegis of A. H. R. (later, Sir Roy) Fedden. This engine design was first test-run in September 1934 and soon produced a maximum power of 500hp. Though no authority was granted for immediate construction of a prototype, Barnwell's brainchild was designated as Bristol Type 135, and its obvious potential created great enthusiasm within the company. However, by a fortuitous coincidence, the proprietor of the national newspaper *Daily Mail*, Lord Rothermere, an ardent advocate of British aviation, during an editorial luncheon discussion on the current state of civil aviation, declared his intention of having 'the fastest commercial aeroplane in Europe' built to his private order; primarily to counteract the lavish contemporary claims by America for its Douglas DC-1. The editor of the *Bristol Evening World*, Robert T. Lewis, quickly informed Rothermere of the potential of the Bristol Type 135, and was accordingly given one week to obtain all particulars of the design.

On 6 March 1934 Frank Barnwell gave Lewis an estimated all-out speed of 240mph at 6,500ft for the Type 135, provided it was fitted with Bristol Mercury engines instead of Aquilas, and incorporated moderate supercharging. Lewis promptly passed this estimate to Rothermere, then on 26 March telephoned Roy Fedden to tell him that Rothermere wished to have the Type 135 built for his private use. In fact, this firm order created mild apprehension among the Bristol Company's directors. Rothermere had a well-deserved reputation as a 'crusader' both in journalism and in politics, albeit with strong

Below:
Father-figure. Bristol Type 142, *Britain First*, serialled K7557, flying from RAF Martlesham Heath on test, 1936. *Flight International*

Above:
Bristol Type 142 in its original form, with four-blade wooden airscrews, Filton, April 1935.
British Aerospace

Right:
Bristol Type 143 (two 500hp Aquilas), registered as G-ADEK, which first flew on 20 January 1936.

Below:
Bristol Type 143 about to taxy. *Flight International*

nationalistic motives. His given reasons for ordering the Type 135 included a desire to promote civil aviation amongst British business firms, but also provided him with 'ammunition' to 'fire' at the Air Ministry by producing a high-speed transport aircraft which could outpace existing RAF fighters and light bombers. Since the Air Ministry was the Bristol Aeroplane Company's best 'customer', the possibility of offending Air Ministry officialdom by undertaking the press baron's private order had to be taken into consideration. A luncheon meeting between Rothermere and the company's hierarchy took place in London on 29 March, during the course of which Rothermere stipulated his requirements of the aircraft, and promised to pay £18,500 for its construction; half this sum immediately the contract was signed, and the remaining half in 12 months time, provided the aircraft was flying by then.

The company's directors next approached the Air Ministry and, as tactfully as possible, outlined Rothermere's request. To their relief the Air Ministry expressed enthusiasm for such a project, and plans were put in hand immediately to proceed with construction. Though the Air Ministry remained an interested 'spectator' only at this stage, its enthusiasm for the basic design almost certainly encouraged Barnwell to bear in mind the possibility of later conversion of his design for RAF use. As a result it was decided to build not only Rothermere's Type 135, but also a twin-Aquila engined prototype variant which would readily utilise up to 70% of the 135's components. With twin Mercury engines in

Above:
Captain Frank Sowter Barnwell, OBE, AFC, BSc. *BAe*

Below:
Two views of the Blenheim I prototype, K7033 (as yet unmarked) at Filton, June 1936.

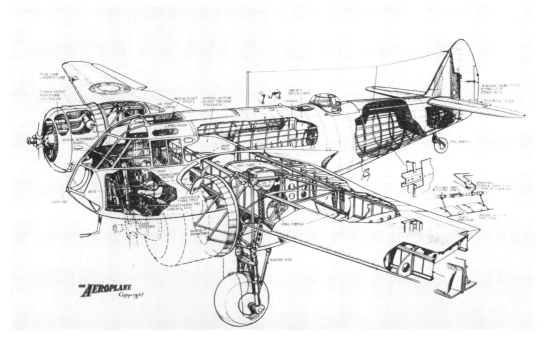

Above:
Production Blenheim I of the second production batch on pre-delivery (to RAF) air-test, 1938. *BAe*

Left:
Plug-in. Early delivery Mk I to 90 Squadron at Bicester.
MoD(Air)

Below:
Blenheim I, K7037 first issued to 114 Squadron on 17 March 1937, and later served as '90-B', 90 Squadron in 1938.

place of the originally intended Aquilas, the Type 135 became retitled as Type 142; while the projected Aquila-powered variant about to be built in parallel became Type 143. This latter had its fuselage slightly enlarged to accommodate eight passengers and a crew of two pilots, while its nose profile was sharper than that of the 142. Foreign interest in the Type 143 — in particular, Finland — was quickly indicated, especially in a possible militarised version having Mercury VI engines, designated Type 143F by the Bristol designers, which could easily be adapted for a variety of military roles and could (on paper, at least) be armed with a forward-firing 20mm Madsen 'cannon' and a dorsal 'free' Lewis machine gun mounting. Negotiations by the Finnish government for provision of nine 143Fs began in February 1935, but on 12 April 1935 the Type 142 made its first flight at Filton, with greatly promising results. The Air Ministry's close interest in the design immediately brought a letter from the Chief of Air Staff, RAF who commented:

'... I agree ... that the Bristol twin should be considered as a medium bomber if Bristols have a reasonable proposition to put forward for the supply of this type in reasonable numbers. In this connection I suggest that we should offer to test the air-craft made for Lord Rothermere at Martlesham free of charge in order to ascertain its performance and characteristics'.

Though the Type 142 had been civil-registered as 'G-ADCZ on 25 February 1935, it never carried this marking. Instead, already privately named *Britain First*, the aircraft bore the experimental marking R-12 when it arrived at RAF Martlesham in June 1935, having been given to the Air Ministry by its owner, Rothermere. In July it received the serial K7557, and in October its civil registration was officially cancelled.

At Martlesham Rothermere's gift-aircraft underwent Service trials and produced impressive performance figures of 285mph with maximum load, and a top speed of 307mph; figures indicating that it was some 15-20% faster than any contemporary firstline RAF fighter. By July 1935 its makers proposed a bomber version, titled Type 142M, which entailed bringing the wing to mid-fuselage — thereby permitting incorporation of an under-fuselage bomb bay — and the installation of a dorsal gun turret for defensive purposes. Modification of the nose compartment permitted a bomb aimer's compartment; while the tailplane and elevators were raised by some eight inches. These, and other minor internal rearrangements, were incorporated in AM Specification B28/35, drawn up in August 1935, followed in September by a contract for production of 150 aircraft with the name Blenheim I. The prototype Blenheim I, serialled K7033, made its initial flight on 25 June 1936, and after Service trials at Martlesham had been successfully completed the design was

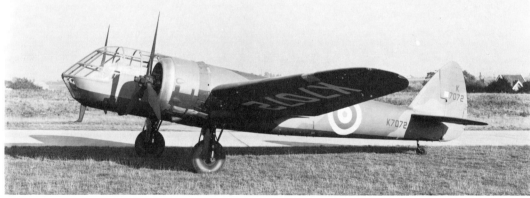

Top left:
Revised nose section for Blenheim IV, Filton, December 1937. *BAe*

Centre left:
Completed K7072 'prototype' Bolingbroke, October 1937. *BAe*

Bottom left:
K7072 with the definitive Mk IV nose section, Filton, 28 December 1937. *BAe*

Above:
Production lines of Blenheim Is at Filton, Bristol.
via J. W. R. Taylor

Left:
Mk IV Blenheim production prewar.

given official 'go ahead' for production in December 1936.

Meantime, *Britain First* (K7557) continued to be modified in minor ways, completed further trials at Martlesham, and was then sent to the Royal Aircraft Establishment, Farnborough where it undertook various semi-hack duties until 1942, and was then relegated to No 10 School of Technical Training, Kirkham with the Instructional Airframe serial 2211M. It was eventually scrapped at Cowley on 1944. Its 'twin brother', the Type 143, registered as G-ADEK on 22 March 1935, did not make its first flight until 20 January 1936. It was retained at Filton, and ultimately scrapped some four years later. The excellence of the Type 142 design ensured the birth of the Blenheim bomber; even to the extent of production contracts for the bomber version being confidently placed by officialdom before the prototype had completed any traditionally lengthy development programme — in short, 'straight off the drawing board'. Such faith (and foresight) by officialdom was no small tribute to the genius of the aircraft's chief designer, Frank Sowter Barnwell OBE, AFC, BSc. Though he lived to see the first Blenheims enter firstline RAF service, Barnwell was to die at the controls of a privately-designed monoplane in a crash on 2 August 1938. Of the many tributes accorded to Barnwell after his tragic death, perhaps the most succinct was that of one contemporary: 'No other designer has turned out so many first class aeroplanes which have become historic'.

Top:
Mk IVs of second production batch at Filton, 23 April 1939. N6161 went to 114 Squadron and was lost in France, May 1940, while N6167 went to 59 Squadron. BAe

Above:
Four N-serial Mk IVs off production lines, at Filton, April 1939. BAe

Below:
Mk IV, L4842 being test-flown by Bill Pegg near Filton on 29 May 1939. This machine went to 53 Squadron and was lost in action on 17 May 1940. BAe

2
Into Service

As one facet of 'Scheme C', the first of several major (and rather hasty) expansion programmes for the RAF in the late 1930s, factory production of Blenheim I bombers commenced with an initial order contract for 150 aircraft (RAF serials K7034-K7182 inc) issued to Bristol's Filton works on 22 August 1935. Succeeding revised Schemes, eg 'F' and 'L', quickly enlarged the aircraft production totals required for the RAF; this rapid escalation being in direct parallel to the looming prospects of a major war in Europe as Hitler's demands for more Germanic territories (*Lebensraum*) became increasingly bolder. The first indications of such ascending production in the context of the Blenheim came in July 1936, when a second order for 434 more machines was placed (L1097-L1530), and this number was then increased by a further 134 aircraft (L1531-

L1546; L4817-L4934); all of these scheduled for delivery to the RAF. By early 1937 factory production of Blenheim Is was far advanced, and on 10 March 1937 the fourth production machine to leave the assembly lines, K7036, was delivered by air to RAF Wyton as the intended start of replacements for No 114 Squadron's outdated Hawker Hinds and Audaxes. Unfortunately, its pilot over-applied the Blenheim's brakes on landing; K7036 flipped over, broke its back and was an immediate write-off. Within the next few weeks, however, No 114 Squadron received a full complement of Blenheim Is and conversion training of the unit's crews was well under way.

For RAF pilots accustomed only to biplanes with fixed undercarriages, open cockpits, lack of brakes, fixed pitch airscrews, etc, the change to metal

Below:
Blenheim I, K7036 first to be delivered to the RAF, crashed at Wyton, 10 March 1937 on arrival for 114 Squadron. *via P. H. T. Green*

Bottom:
Blenheim IV, N6155 of 114 Squadron, Wyton, 1939; eventually struck-off RAF charge on 4 April 1940. *Imperial War Museum (IWM)*

monocoque monoplanes, enclosed cockpits, variable pitch airscrews, rectractable undercarriages, safety flaps and other innovations came as something of a shock. Perhaps inevitably, a number of the early deliveries suffered varying degrees of 'self-inflicted' damage in the hands of unpractised pilots, necessitating, at worst, total replacement or at least lengthy grounding undergoing repairs in unit hangars. The experience of Plt Off (later, Wg Cdr, DSO, DFC) Dave Penman at that period was not entirely uncommon:

'I joined 44 Squadron in October 1938 after completing training on Tiger Moth, Hart and Audax. The squadron was equipped with 18 Mk I Blenheims but very few were fit to fly due to a shortage of spares. I had no experience of twin-engined aircraft, retracting undercarriages, flaps, variable pitch airscrews or high speed. Consequently it was quite a thrill to fly a Blenheim! This was a very fast aircraft for its time, cruising at 180mph. It had a blind flying panel, thus giving me my first sight of an artificial horizon . . . dual instruction was minimal; a few circuits with the Flight Commander, a little flying with one engine throttled back, and you were on your own. Flying itself was limited because of the shortage of serviceable aircraft, and I had around 10 hours flying

on the Blenheim when I was given the squadron's least serviceable aircraft for a short cross-country ar I jokingly told to break it! Low cloud made the cross-country a bit tricky as I had no real cloud-flying experience, and a number of accidents involving Blenheims diving into the ground out of cloud made one wary of going on to instruments. Arriving back at base, all went well until the approach to land. When more power was required the port engine stopped. With the starboard engine going well, the aircraft rapidly dropped a wing and went out of control. I shall never forget looking down the port wing to see the propeller stopped as the wingtip dug into the ground and the aircraft cartwheeled. Fortunately, it fell the right way up. The engines broke off and the fuselage split at the turret and slid to a halt. The gunner fell out of the fuselage on to the grass and was unhurt. I got out of the cockpit with my observer and, walking back to the hangar, met Wg Cdr John Boothman who asked what the joke was — I must have been laughing, perhaps at doing

Below:
Blenheim Is and aircrews of 90 Squadron, Bicester, (OC, Sqn Ldr G. J. C. Paul, 11th from left), late 1938.
Flight International

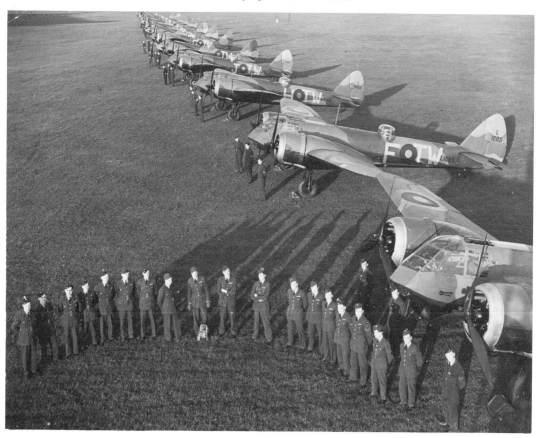

what I was told to do, break it! The accident itself attracted little attention as the Blenheim's engines, Bristol Mercurys, were prone to sudden stoppage — and most accidents were fatal'.*

Notwithstanding this minor crop of damaging accidents, the smooth production flow of new machines from the various factories ensured ready replacement and the planned re-equipment of RAF squadrons during 1937-38 continued apace. Following the lead of 114 Squadron came Nos 90, 139, 144, 110 and 44 Squadrons during the remaining months of 1937, in that sequence of initial deliveries of Blenheim Is. In 1938 further units to receive the type were — again, in sequence of initial deliveries — Nos 61, 62, 82, 57, 104, 108, 101, 34, 21, 107 and 600 Squadron, Auxiliary Air Force (AAF) — all commencing re-equipment by the end of September 1938 and thus totalling 17 UK-based squadrons of Blenheim Is on the eve of that month's Munich crisis, when Britain was poised on the brink of possible war with Hitler's Third Reich. In addition, in January 1938, the first Blenheim I to go to an overseas-based RAF unit went to No 30 Squadron, based at Dhibban, Iraq (renamed Habbaniya on

*'44 Squadron on Operations'; A. N. White, 1977.

25 March 1938). In December 1938 four more units received their first Blenheim Is, Nos 23, 29, 25 and 64 Squadrons. All four of these units, along with 600 Squadron AAF, received Blenheim IF variants; standard production Mk Is 'converted' to fighters by the relatively simple addition of an external pack containing four fixed, forward-firing 0.303in Browning machine guns under the bomb bay compartment.

In 1939, as war with Germany gradually became a distinct possibility, Blenheim Is continued to be issued to RAF units as replacements for outmoded designs still in firstline use. In the UK four more squadrons received Mk Is or IFs, ie Nos 53, 601 AAF, 18 and 59 (in date sequence); while no less than nine overseas-based RAF units also took

Below
Blenheim I, L1132, OZ-L of 82 Squadron, 1939. Note under-fuselage Light Series bomb-carriers for practice bombing. *Major Rice*

Bottom:
Formation from 90 Squadron (with TW-codes 'censored').

deliveries of Mk Is. Of these 84 Squadron at Shaibah, Iraq received its first example on 17 February 1939. Further east, No 60 Squadron, based at Ambala in northern India, had its latest appointed Commanding Officer, Sqn Ldr (later, AVM, CB, AFC) S. R. Ubee AFC arrived on 7 March flying the unit's first Blenheim I which he had 'collected' from 30 Squadron en route. A sister unit in India, No 39, exchanged its Westland Wapitis for Blenheims later in the year. In May 1939 Nos 8 (Khormaksar, Aden), 55 (Habbaniyah) and 211 (Ismailia, Egypt) commenced 'conversion' to Blenheim Is; then, on 1 June, No 113 Squadron at Heliopolis, Egypt received its first Blenheim I, as did 45 Squadron (Ismailia) later in that month. At Tengah, Singapore, in July, No 11 Squadron began accepting its quota of Blenheim Is. While an obvious

need for 'modern' aircraft designs was plainly evident among many UK-based squadrons in 1939, it was doubly necessary for virtually all RAF units based abroad, most of which were still soldiering on with obsolete biplanes of increasing vintage.

Another overt 'gap' in the UK-based Fighter Command defence system was the complete lack of any specifically designed fighter for night interception of any aerial invader. The immediate compromise solution was a virtual ad hoc 'conversion' of several day fighter designs to 'night-fighters', albeit in most cases with little additional provision for such a specialised role. Among these was the Blenheim IF 'fighter', which formed the initial equipment of 11 squadrons, all reformed in October 1939 — Nos 92, 145, 219, 222, 229, 234, 236, 242, 245, 248 and 254. In most cases, however, these units merely worked up to operational status on the Blenheims, then exchanged these for Hurricanes or Spitfires before commencing actual operational work. Nevertheless, the Blenheim IF played a pioneering role in the development of Airborne Interception (AI) radar for night-fighters. The conception of airborne radar (a term not generally used until 1943, being known initially as Radio Direction Finding, or RDF) came in early 1936 when Robert Watson-Watt and his team of the Radio Department of the National Physical Laboratory put forward such a project for consideration. Experimental airborne transmitters were tested in late 1937, with some success, and by the close of 1938 AI sets were being contracted for production. The AOC-in-C Fighter Command,

Hugh Dowding, who had taken part in one AI trial as an observer, gave his shrewd opinion that AI could best be utilised in future in twin-engined aircraft with a two-man crew; a prediction which proved prophetic.

The selection of the Blenheim IF as the pioneering operational night-fighter was not simply a random choice. Admittedly, the original decision to convert Mk I Blenheim bombers into 'long-range escort fighters' (sic) by the Air Ministry in late 1938 — thus 'creating' the Mk IF variant — was not allied to their use for night-fighting. Contracts for the production of four-gun belly packs for the proposed Mk IFs were placed with the Southern Railway's Ashford, Kent works, eventually producing more than 1,300 gun packs, the first such order being for 200 packs. These four-gun packs, bolted under the Blenheim's bomb bay, each contained 2,000 rounds of belted 0.303in calibre ammunition (500 rounds per gun); sufficient for at least 20 seconds continuous firing. It might be noted here too that the later orders for gun packs were for conversion of Blenheim Mk IVs to Mk IVFs. In December 1938 the first Mk IF Blenheims entered service with No 25 Squadron, based then at Hawkinge; the first example being flown in on 10 December. The decision to fit AI radar to Blenheim IFs came in a secret minute dated 17 July 1939 from the Air Ministry, which called for 21 Blenheim IFs to be so equipped 'as quickly as possible' (sic). These AI sets were quickly delivered

Right:
No 21 Squadron line-up at Watton, 1939. Nearest, L1345, later used by 90 and 104 Squadrons, 13 OTU, then went to Finland on 21 February 1940; next, L1350 (later 90 Squadron); L1363, which flew with 90, 104, 88 and 526 Squadrons and was ultimately discovered crashed at Morveen on 19 October 1943.
via RAF Museum

Below:
Blenheim IF, L1426 of 25 Squadron during August 1939 'wargames'. It later crashed at Northolt on 17 December 1939.

by Pye & Metrovick factories to the Royal Aircraft Establishment (RAE) at Farnborough where actual installation was undertaken, and aircraft deliveries to No 25 Squadron began on 31 July 1939 — the world's first operational radar-fitted night-fighters. By 3 September 1939 — the outbreak of World War 2 — 15 AI Mk IFs had been delivered to 25 Squadron, and the next six had arrived on the unit before the end of the month.

While production of Blenheim Is was aimed at supplying RAF requirements only from the outset in 1936, once the initial factory orders were well under way, the Bristol Company was permitted to start very limited export orders for foreign countries. The first requests from foreign governments for Type 142Ms had come from Finland and Lithuania in 1935, for 10 aircraft and eight aircraft respectively. With Air Ministry approval — once RAF needs had been satisfied — the manufacturers eventually negotiated contracts with Finland for 18 machines in March 1936, and with Turkey for 12 machines in April. The Finnish contract was finalised in October 1936 for 18 Blenheim Is, adapted to carry non--British armament, and the allotted batch, serialled BL104-BL121 inclusive, began leaving the Bristol Filton works from July 1937. On 12 April 1938 the Finnish government acquired a licence to build Blenheims in a new *Valtion Lentokonetehdas* (State Aircraft Factory) at Tampere, though in the event no Finnish-built Blenheims had been completed before November 1939 when the Russo-Finnish 'Winter War' erupted. Yugoslavia also acquired a licence to manufacture Blenheims to a total of 50 machines, and purchased two 'sample' aircraft which were ferried in November 1937, bearing British civil registrations G-AFCE and G-AFCF. The Turkish government initially ordered 12 machines, the first pair being despatched by sea in October 1937, and 10 more, bearing British civil registrations G-AFFP to G-AFFZ, were flown out between March and June 1938. A second batch of 18 Blenheims Is, civil-registered G-AFLA to G-AFLS, were flown to Turkey in small numbers between November 1938 and February 1939.

Once the initial Blenheim I design was 'off the drawing board' the Bristol Co immediately looked to future developments and fresh designs. Following an

Below:
Believed line-up of 139 Squadron, prewar. Nearest, L1100, later used by 35, 40 and 101 Squadrons and 13 OTU. *V. F. Bingham*

Bottom:
K7054, 'F', of 90 Squadron, 1938.

Air Ministry Specification G24/35, issued in August 1935 requiring a future replacement for the Avro Anson and its coastal reconnaissance role, the company tendered what amounted to a slightly 'fatter' version of the Blenheim I titled as Type 149. Though not accepted by officialdom as such, this project, combined with a land-based torpedo-bomber requirement under AM Spec M15/35, resulted in a fresh specification, 10/36, which led to the Bristol Type 152 later emerging as the Bristol Beaufort. In the interim the Air Ministry expressed its approval for a 'stop gap' general reconnaissance development of the Blenheim I, to which the Type 149 titling was transferred by the designers. In the interests of ease of production this Type 149 utilised most Mk I components, but the characteristic nose 'glasshouse' was extended forward by some three feet to provide accommodation for a navigator-cum-bomb aimer; while the wings outboard of engines were modified to accept extra fuel tankage in order to provide greater range performance. A production Blenheim I, K7072, became the prototype machine for this Type 149 and was initially freshly named as the Bristol Bolingbroke I.

In its original extended-nose configuration K7072 was first air-tested on 24 September 1937 with Cyril F. Uwins at its controls. On landing, Uwins

Right:
K7046 of 114 Squadron seen at Wyton during rehearsal for 1937 Empire Air Day. *Flight International*

Below:
L1304, which served with 110 Squadron from 1 September 1938 to 18 September 1939 before being relegated to instructional duties. *via P. H. T. Green*

Above:
Trio from 44 Squadron, Waddington, May 1938. Nearest, K7133, 'L' later served with 144,145 and 604 Squadrons, and was eventually SOC on 1 October 1943. *BAe*

Below:
Ground view of K7133, 'L' of 44 Squadron at Waddington, May 1938. Note under-fuselage Light Series bomb carriers. *BAe*

Top:
Dinghy Drill. Air Gunner of Blenheim I, 'B' of 90 Squadron, Bicester, demonstrating method of throwing out the crew dinghy in the event of any 'ditching', 1938. *Flight International*

Above left:
K7092, 'K' (also TW–J) of 90 Squadron, which later served with 23 Squadron. *MoD (Air)*

Above right:
K7040, 'V' (ex-114 Squadron) and K7060 (ex-139 Squadron) serving as instructional machines for aircraft apprentices at Halton, 1939. *via C. C. H. Cole*

expressed dissatisfaction with the lengthy glasshouse nose as interfering seriously with a pilot's forward vision. Accordingly, the nose section was redesigned to give the pilot a normal close windscreen, while the transparent roof of the navigator/bomb aimer compartment was lowered below the pilot's natural eye-line. Even so, this revision continued to obstruct forward vision, particularly for landing, and further modification resulted in a curved scalloping profile along the port side of the forward compartment. In this form the type was accepted for production in mid-1938. Once normal production of this long-nose

Above:
First to receive Mk IVs was 53 Squadron, seen here at Odiham, 1939. Nearest, L4841, TE-N was lost in action on 18 May 1940. *Grp Capt J. Butterworth*

version was found to be practicable without interrupting existing Mk I production, the name Bolingbroke was dropped and the new variant became titled Blenheim Mk IV. As such it was adopted for licence production in Canada for RCAF use, where the name Bolingbroke was revived and applied to aircraft produced by Fairchild Aircraft Ltd of Longueuil, Quebec. The initial contract placed with Fairchild by the Canadian Department of National Defence was for 18 aircraft for 'coastal reconnaissance', and was worth some $1\frac{1}{2}$ million dollars.

Production of the more powerfully engined, longer range Mk IV began to supersede that of Mk Is by the close of 1938, and in January 1939 the first Mk IVs issued to the RAF went to No 53 Squadron, based at Odiham, an army cooperation unit, while on 22 March 1939 the first Mk IV bomber example to reach an RAF firstline unit, L4865, arrived at Bicester on delivery to No 90 Squadron as the start of replacements for the unit's Mk Is. While the first Mk IVs to leave the production lines were in essence modified Mk I structures incorporating the longer nose and added wing fuel tankage, the eventual 'pure'

built Mk IVs became titled Mk IVL to differentiate these from the early batches. A further title amendment was applied when standard Mk IVs were fitted with underbelly four-gun packs to enable their use as 'fighters', this variant being termed Mk IVF. The first IVF into RAF unit service went to No 25 Squadron in August 1939, intended for night-fighting duties.

The significance of the Blenheims to the RAF in 1939 may be judged by reference to actual quantities of aircraft on RAF charge — in all categories — on 3 September 1939, the first day of war with Nazi Germany. In a breakdown of RAF strength that day by aircraft type, Blenheims were the most numerous available; an overall total of 1,089 (all marks). Of this total, 626 were Mk Is in the UK (including 111 Mk IFs in squadron use) and a further 273 overseas; while Mk IVs on charge, all in the UK, totalled 190 aircraft. In this context of numerical quantities, the Blenheim's nearest 'rivals' were the obsolete Fairey Battle (1,014 aircraft), then the Avro Anson (760); while its contemporary 'brothers' in Bomber Command were Hampdens (212), Whitleys (196) and Wellingtons (175). Despite this clear supremacy in sheer numbers, it should be recognised that the bulk of Blenheims on RAF charge were the Mk I versions, already obsolescent for any projected bombing offensive against Germany.

3
Developments

Apart from a projected Blenheim III version — a long-nose, short range possibility which never achieved production status — the main variant after the Mks I and IV was the Mk V, as it eventually became designated. In line with the contemporary concentration on the employment of light and medium bombers for close tactical support of the army, the Bristol Co proposed in January 1940 a specialised derivation of the Blenheim for just such duties, though with alternative duties as a 'low level fighter' or dual-control trainer. The Air Ministry responded to this proposal with AM Specification B6/40 which stipulated various roles, including direct army support by dive-bombing, low-level bombing, and similar army co-operation tactical use. Accordingly, the designers proposed to modify a Blenheim IV, titling the result Type 160 and naming it Bisley I. Two prototypes, AD657 and AD661, were quickly contracted for construction at Filton.

In its initial configuration the Bisley I incorporated a fresh long-nose section of 'solid' appearance, containing four fixed, forward-firing 0.303in Browning machine guns, each fed by a total of 1,000 rounds of ammunition apiece; while the dorsal turret was a Type BX, with two Brownings. An improved design of windscreen was fitted, while in view of its intended 'deck level' roles the Bisley's whole cockpit was externally protected by some 600lb weight of detachable armour plate. Further armour-plating was thoughtfully provided for the dorsal air gunner's cockpit-cum-turret. Powerplants were Bristol Mercury XVIs rated for maximum power at ground level. By late 1940, since the evacuation of the Allied armies from France, new thoughts were applied to the future roles of the Bisley, and the official specification now called for high level bombing potential in addition to the low level direct support roles. To allow for this additional task the 'solid' nose section was revised to permit interchangeability of the four-gun battery for a navigating-cum-bomb aiming compartment, with an offset aiming window; while an under-nose, rearward-firing twin Browning Frazer Nash (FN) 54 mounting was added for rear defence. High level bombing versions necessarily were stripped of armour-plating, though the addition thereafter of oxygen and more comprehensive radio equipment more or less made up an equal weight penalty. General strengthening of the wing spar structure was undertaken; engines were changed for

Below:
Two views of Blenheim IV, V6083, FV-B of 13 OTU. It had formerly served as BX-Y, 86 Squadron. *BAe*

Mercury 25s or 30s; and the name Bisley was changed to Blenheim V,* with the prototype AD657 then making its first test flight at Filton on 24 February 1941. Production Mk Vs were ordered soon after.

A total of 944 Mk Vs were constructed (including the two prototypes), all but the initial pair being produced by Rootes Securities Ltd of Blythe Bridge, Staffordshire. Though recognised from the outset as slower and less manoeuvrable than its 'parent' Mk IV, the Blenheim V was considered — by the hierarchy, if not the operational crews — as 'better armed', based on the contemporary judgement of officialdom that any inadequacies in pure performance were more than compensated by additional firepower and armour shielding for the crew etc. It must be said that such a theory found little approval among Blenheim V crews at the 'sharp end'. Slight variants of the Mk V, as produced, included the Mk VD, a tropicalised version which was the most produced version; and the Mk VC, a dual-control trainer. The first frontline units to re-equip with Mk Vs included Nos 13, 18, 114 and 614 Squadrons circa September 1942; these squadrons forming No 326 Wing being prepared for service in conjunction with Allied forces in North Africa in the wake of Operation 'Torch'. In early November 1942 the Wing moved to Blida, Algeria and commenced army support operations shortly after, but the

*The name Bisley was *officially* discarded by the Air Ministry on 8 January 1942.

Blenheim V's operational inadequacies quickly became apparent when opposed by Luftwaffe fighters and highly experienced Afrika Korps 88mm flak ground gunners. Casualties mounted swiftly, exemplified perhaps by a sortie led by Wg Cdr Hugh Malcolm of No 18 Squadron on 4 December (see chapter 10). Nevertheless, Mk Vs continued on operations in the Middle East until March-April 1943 before being exchanged (mainly) for Douglas Bostons.

Two other squadrons in the Middle East theatre to receive Mk Vs were Nos 244 and 454 RAAF. The latter, based in Iraq, then Egypt, flew the type only briefly in reconnaissance duties from November 1942 to approx February 1943, when it received Martin Baltimores. No 244 Squadron, however, began receiving Mk Vs in October 1942 for maritime duties around the Gulf of Oman, and was destined to soldier on with the type (mainly) until the eventual arrival of Wellingtons in early 1944. Blenheim Vs were also sent to the Far East operational theatres, though in limited numbers and not always fully equipping individual squadrons.

As with all major aircraft designs intended for Service use in the late 1930s and early 1940s, the basic aircraft design for the Blenheim was the subject of various 'one-off' experimental trials and fitments. Blenheim I, L1348 became an early attempt to produce a high-speed (sic) photo-reconnaissance aircraft, having its gun turret removed, all bomb door and other apertures carefully taped, wingtips

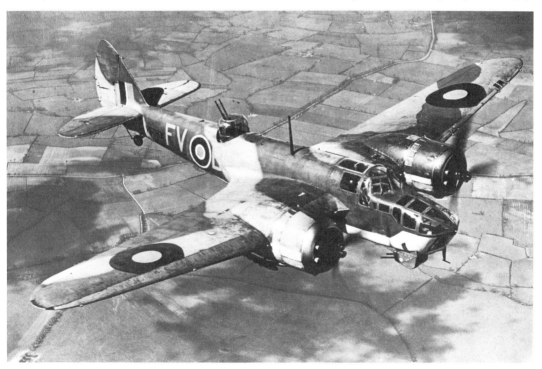

Above and left:
Views of AD657, the Bisley I prototype, July 1941. *BAe*

specially faired and an overall 'polishing' of surfaces. Rotol constant speed airscrews were fitted, and the aircraft given a smooth sky-blue livery. Resulting trials, however, nullified further development of a 'PR' Blenheim per se. Another interesting idea was to provide the aircraft with a tricycle undercarriage, with Blenheim I, L1242 being fitted with a fixed nose wheel. Yet another modification experimentally was the fitting of a hemispherical nose radome to Blenheim IV, L4888 in connection with centimetric radar tests.*

Much trial and no little ingenuity went into a variety of official — and unofficial — attempts to increase the offensive and defensive armament of Blenheims. Mention has been made of the official four-gun belly packs fitted to 'F' versions of Mk Is and IVs; also the undernose, rearward-firing FN54 gun mountings. Additional 'local' ideas in No 2 Group included positioning Vickers Gas-Operated

*Of these 'one off' experimental trials aircraft L1242, having seen service with No 34 Squadron, was eventually SOC (Struck off Charge) on 9 April 1941; L1348 served with No 88 Squadron before being SOC on 12 June 1941; and L4888 saw service with Nos 101 and 35 Squadrons and No 17 OTU and was finally SOC on 7 December 1943.

(VGO) machine guns in the tail and the rear sections of engine nacelles; while a single, gimbal-mounted VGO could often be seen in the nose sections of many squadron Mk IVs. Heavier fire-power fitments were exemplified by locally modified Mk IVs of Nos 114 Squadron RAF and 15 Squadron SAAF in North Africa. These aircraft had the lower right 'window' of the bomb aimer's nose compartment removed to permit installation of a single Hispano 20mm cannon, for low-level strafing operations. An even heavier weapon, the 37mm Coventry Ordnance Works (COW) cannon, was fitted on a trial basis in Blenheim I, L6594 at Boscombe Down, rigged between the spars and firing vertically downwards, with the purpose of providing an effective anti-submarine strike weapon. The thornier problem of increasing the Blenheim's effective bombload was a far from simple proposition. Little could be done to enlarge the basic bomb bay accommodation — usually accepting four 250lb bombs only — though very minor modifications at squadron level often enabled 'mixed' loads of GP bombs and 40lb 'anti-personnel' fragmentation stores to be carried. External bomb carriers, fitted under the inner wing sections, could offer the lift of two additional 250lb bombs, though only with precautionary strengthening of undercarriage; a trial fitment was added to the projected Mk II variant, and used on occasion with

31

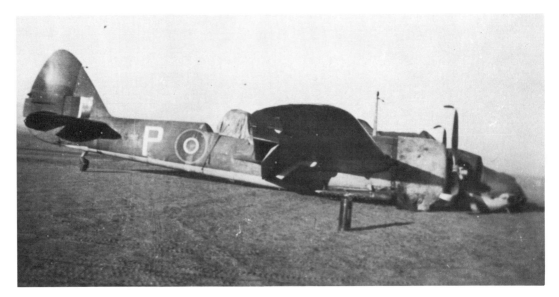

Above:
Blenheim V, believed of 614 Squadron (?).

Left:
40 Squadron Blenheim being bombed up with 250lb GP bombs.

Below:
Checking a mixed load of 40lb HE and 4lb Incendiary bombs in a Middle East Blenheim.

Top right:
The under-fuselage Light Series carriers commonly used by Blenheims.

later Mk IVs. For anti-shipping operations such bomb loads became mixtures of AS (anti-submarine) bombs or depth charges, but the size of the Blenheim's standard bomb bay precluded carriage of torpedoes, despite several 'one-off' attempts to carry same. In the event it was left to a Blenheim successor, the Beaufort, to become a principal torpedo-bomber; while a further 'child', the pugnacious Beaufighter, was also to do sterling work in the field of maritime strike duties.

In its original publicity brochure for the Blenheim I, the Bristol Aeroplane Co described the bomb bay et al in the following terms:

'All bombs are carried internally on the centre of gravity of the machine in a bomb cell under the centre plane. Hinged doors cover the bomb cells, these doors being of double-skin construction for torsional stiffness. They are opened by the weight of the falling bombs and closed by return springs. Various types of bombs can be accommodated and for this purpose two Universal carriers are attached to the supports provided in the bomb cells. Detachable inspection panels are also provided on the sides of the fuselage.'

'A hand winch has been devised for loading. This takes the form of a geared cable winder, which operates from inside the body through the roof of the bomb compartment. The winch registers over the centre of each carrier and the cable is dropped through the floor of the body on each side of the carrier. Hooks on these cables pick up a belly band under the bomb, when the bomb can be raised up to the hook by operating the winch. If the bomb hook does not register exactly into the release unit, the winch can be rocked sideways, causing the bomb to roll slightly until able to enter the release catch. Observation holes are provided in the roof of the

bomb cells so that the operator inside can see the raising of the bombs and also communicate with the helper outside. After hooking the bomb, the stays, etc, can be adjusted through large hand-holes provided in the side and centre walls of the bomb compartments. Provision is also made for hoisting small bombs in pairs on special racks.'

'Cells for four small sighter or Practice bombs of 20lb each are provided in the outer wing or for the carrying of flares. Provision is also made for carrying additional Practice bombs or reconnaissance flares under the fuselage aft of the bomb cell. A "Jettison Lamp" is provided in the bomb control station, which can be used to indicate that the various bomb circuits are intact. The "Jettison Lamp" is switched on before each bomb is released, and it is extinguished when the bomb actually falls. All bombs can be released together in case of emergency.'

While quoting that brochure, the explanation of the pilot's only 'offensive armament' is of interest:

'. . . consists of a fixed forward gun mounted in the port wing and fired by the pilot. The fixed gun is mounted on a detachable cradle in the outer wing on the port side, outside the airscrew disc. The belt box is removable for reloading, access to this and the gun being by means of a detachable panel underneath the wing. The pilot's gunsight for the fixed gun is in the nose of the aircraft offset to the port side of the centre line. The foresight is fixed, and for the rear sight, which can be folded when not in use, vertical adjustment is provided. A camera gun can also be fitted under the front fuselage, if required.'

It might be noted that in that original description the pilot's gun was a Vickers machine gun; while the rear dorsal turret armament was stated to be a Lewis gun.

4
Exports

Foreign interest in the Blenheim began even before the design appeared as such, when Finland commenced overtures to obtain both civil and military variants of the Bristol Type 143 in mid-1934. With these in mind the Bristol Co prepared a brochure for a Type 143F version, powered by Mercury VI engines, with interchangeable nose and rear fuselage sections to cope with a range of civil and military roles. For its projected fighter-bomber use the design incorporated provision for a forward 20mm Madsen cannon and a mid-upper Lewis gun mounting. Negotiations for the supply of nine aircraft to Type 143F standard commenced in February 1935, only to be nullified when the British Air Ministry expressed a firm interest in development of the Type 142 as a day-bomber, resulting in the parent company committing its production capacity to the Air Ministry as a first priority, though with a reservation that any future orders from outside the UK could be accepted with British governmental approval. Despite this setback, Finland remained determined to obtain Blenheims, as witnessed by its acquiring a licence to manufacture Blenheims in

April 1938. The subsequent history of the Finnish Blenheims is detailed in the next chapter.

A second foreign government to obtain such a licence was that of Yugoslavia. This licence allowed for the building of 50 machines by the Ikarus AD at Zemun, but two sample aircraft were first purchased and, in November 1937, ferried out carrying the civil registrations G-AFCE and G-AFCF. Within less than a year of obtaining construction plans the Ikarus works began manufacture and in the event had completed 16 machines by early 1941 when Germany invaded the Balkans. This latter event caused Yugoslav patriots to sabotage the Zemun factory to prevent its use by the Germans, destroying 24 other uncompleted Blenheims in the process. Meantime, on 13 February 1940 a total of 20 more Blenheims were withdrawn from RAF charge and flown from Aston Down to Zemun. These were L6813, L6814 and L6817-L6834 inc, though for the ferry flight were marked in civil registrations YU-BAA to YU-BAT inc. The subsequent fate of most of these Yugoslav Blenheims is sketchily recorded. On 7 April 1941, for example, the Yugoslav Air Force attacked several Hungarian towns along the southern border. Nine of the raiders were shot down; six of these were known to be Blenheims of which four were brought down by German fighters and the other two were victims of

Below:
Blenheim I, L-104 in Hungarian livery, April 1941 at Budaörs.

Above:
Blenheim I in Turkish markings, 1938.

Hungarian flak. At least one Yugoslav Air Force Blenheim, flown by a pilot of Hungarian nationality, was deliberately landed in Hungary and surrendered. This aircraft, a Blenheim I, landed in April 1941 and was re-marked in Hungarian livery with the new serial L-104. It was later modified for transport duties and continued in Hungarian use until nearly the end of the war.

Although licensed production of Blenheims was not undertaken by the Turkish government, the Turkish Air Force was to use a greater quantity of the type than any other foreign service. Its first two examples (Nos 8155 and 8156) were sent by sea in October 1937, while between March and June 1938 a further 10 aircraft (Nos 8157-8166) were flown out bearing civil registrations G-AFFP and G-AFFR to G-AFFZ inc. A further batch of 18 (Nos 9222-9239) were flown out between November 1938 and February 1939, marked G-AFLA to G-AFLP, G-AFLR and G-AFLS. During the following three years at least 26 more Blenheims were diverted to the Turkish Air Force. On 21 September 1939 nine Blenheims were sent (L1483, L1485, L1488, L1489, L1493, L4821, L4824, L4826 and L4828), the first five of these being ex-211 Squadron RAF machines, and the rest other ex-RAF squadron aircraft.

Other Blenheims known to have been transferred to Turkey — mainly ex-RAF squadron aircraft — included T1996, Z7986, BA137, BA292, BA395, BA488, BA495, BA591, BA613, BA614, BA713, BA854, BA855, BA887, BA910, BA922 and BA925.

A close 'rival' for Turkey in the context of the largest quantitative user of Blenheims outside the UK was Rumania. At least 39 Blenheims were sent to the Rumanian Air Force prior to the outbreak of World War 2 in 1939, in the following batches:

```
17 May — L8619, L8620
13 June — L8603-L8608 inc
20 June — L8622, L8624-L8630, L8632,
          L8652-L8654
26 June — L6696-L6708 inc; L6713-L6718 inc
```

In November 1939, as part of a diplomatic ploy hoping to persuade Rumania to join the Allies

Above:
One of 12 Mk IVs, in temporary civil registrations, delivered to the Royal Hellenic Air Force 1939-40. *BAe*

Left:
Blenheim V, BA613 with the Turkish Air Force.

against Germany, a further batch of 13 Blenheims were sent to Rumania. In the event Rumania joined the Axis powers a year later, and by June 1941 was at war with Russia. Some Rumanian Blenheims were still in frontline use, albeit under Luftwaffe operational control, as late as August 1944.

Greece, a neighbour of Yugoslavia and Rumania, received a total of 18 Blenheims. The first dozen, unarmed and civil-registered G-AFXD to G-AFXO, were delivered to the Royal Hellenic Air Force between 13 October 1939 and 10 February 1940. These went to *32a Mira Vomvardismou* (32nd Bomber Squadron), and were supplemented on 1 April 1941 by six more Blenheims, including L6658, L6670, L8384, and L8385. With the inva-

sion of Greece by first Italy, then Germany, the Greek Blenheims saw close action along the invasion front, scoring several successes in bombing and strafing sorties against Italian objectives. With the entry of German forces however their subsequent activities were both intense and short-lived, sharing a common fate with many of their RAF colleagues in the campaign.

Neutral Portugal, situated close to the main RAF ferrying route to the Mediterranean operational zones, accumulated at least 23 Blenheims at varying periods of the war, some being 'interned' after forced or even crash landings. Known serials include R3623, R2775, R2781, R2799, R3830, T2434, T2431, V5429, V5434, V5501, V5729, V5883, V6395, Z5736, Z5760, Z5762, Z6030, Z6035, Z6341, Z7492, AZ986, AZ987 and BA826. Other 'unintentional' internees included L8837 which crashed at Cintra on 15 September 1943. Portugal was not the only neutral country to 'gain' Blenheims as 'uninvited guests'. Eire, with its proximity to Britain's western coastline, and bordering Northern Ireland, became host to a variety of RAF aircraft

throughout the war including Blenheims K7068 (14 March 1941), L6720 (14 March 1941) and L9415 of 272 Squadron (20 December 1940), N3533 of 143 Squadron (19 April 1942) and No 3610 of 254 Squadron (crashed 12 September 1941). Prior to the German 1940 invasion of its territory, Belgium too had been a neutral, but received a number of 'unsolicited exports' when several RAF aircraft strayed over its borders, including Blenheims L1148 of 57 Squadron (16 November 1939) and L8875 of 18 Squadron (30 April 1940).

While the principal Blenheim IV licensed production in Canada was for the Bolingbroke variant, nine 'normal' Blenheims, albeit intended to have D/F radio modifications, were originally earmarked for the RCAF from a 1938-39 production batch at Filton. In the event none of these went to the RCAF,* though on 19 February 1940 seven Blenheims to RAF standards were officially transferred to the RCAF: L9309, L9311, L9312, L9376, L9377, L9380 and L9384.

In South Africa the need for a modern-equipped air force had finally been recognised from 1934, and in the following year the Minister of Defence,

Oswald Pirow, announced an acceleration of the defence expansion plan, to be completed by 1937 at latest, which would include a squadron of bomber aircraft of up-dated design and a flight of 'super-fighter' (sic) aircraft. He had in mind the Fairey Battle and the Bristol Blenheim for bombers, and the Hawker Hurricane. It was not until early 1939, however, that the first example of a Blenheim appeared in South Africa, and this machine, L1431, was test-flown on 11 March at Cape Town. Three days later it flew from Young's Field, Cape Town, to Waterkloof at an average speed of 242mph. In consequence of this impressive performance, 'large orders' (sic) were negotiated for further Blenheims, but none was ever supplied. At the outbreak of war in Europe the South African Air Force possessed only six truly modern aircraft, ie one Battle, four Mk I Hurricanes (a fifth Hurricane supplied had crashed) and Blenheim L1431. The latter remained with the SAAF until 29 August 1940, on which date it was returned to the RAF and reserialled as AX683.

---

*Four of these, P4856-P4859, have in the past been quoted as 'Delivered to RCAF' whereas all four went to RAF units, two being lost to enemy action in early 1940.

5
Into Battle

From 11.00hrs BST on Sunday, 3 September 1939, Britain was at war with Hitler's Third Reich — and one minute later a Blenheim IV pilot of 139 Squadron based at Wyton, Flg Off Andrew McPherson, a Glaswegian, received orders to take off at noon to reconnoitre the German Fleet in the area of Wilhelmshaven. Accordingly, at 12.03hrs McPherson, accompanied by Cdr Thompson, RN and Cpl V. Arrowsmith in Blenheim IV, N 6215 left the Wyton 'runway' and steadily climbed through haze and freezing mists, eventually reaching a ceiling of some 24,000ft. Reaching the objective, Cdr Thompson began sketching details of ships' locations, while the aircraft camera, after taking 75 photographs, succumbed to the freezing temperatures, as did the Blenheim's radio. The loss of communication prevented any details being relayed to base, where a Blenheim force was standing by for orders to bomb the German Fleet. Finally, at 16.50hrs, the lone Blenheim landed safely back at Wyton, having completed the RAF's first

operational sortie of the war. Next day, despite appalling weather, McPherson, again in N6215, returned to attempt to photograph German shipping in and around Wilhelmshaven, Cuxhaven, Kiel and Brunsbüttel; the weather conditions forcing him to fly at little more than 250ft height over his objectives. Again, he returned safely with his photographs after four gruelling hours at the Blenheim's controls. Without waiting to study McPherson's photos, five Blenheims from each of three squadrons, Nos 107, 110 and 139, took off between 15.30 and 16.00hrs to attack German shipping; the first RAF bombing raid of the conflict.

The target was the Schillig Roads area. After crossing the North Sea through blinding rainstorms, which forced the 15 Blenheims to fly at heights from sea level to no higher than 100ft, the force made landfall at Heligoland as planned, then changed course towards their target. What followed proved both tragic and frustrating. Leading the forward element of 110 Squadron was Flt Lt K. C. Doran in Blenheim N6204, who sighted the *Admiral Scheer* at anchor and promptly attacked, taking the German defences by surprise. One of the 110 Squadron formation (N6199) was lost, but the second wave from 107 Squadron quickly lost four of its five Blenheims (N6184, N6188, N6240 and N6189) to the alerted

Below:
Blenheim IV on patrol.

defenders. The third element, 139 Squadron, simply failed to find the objective and returned to base unscathed. On 2 November 1939 Doran and McPherson were among several RAF men awarded a DFC at a royal investiture at Wyton — the first such RAF awards of the war. Another 'first' for Blenheims occurred on 28 November, when six Blenheim IFs of 601 Squadron AAF were joined with six IFs from 25 Squadron in a daylight strafing attack (no bombs) on the Luftwaffe's seaplane base at Borkum. It meant that all crews undertook a 250-mile flight across the North Sea to their target, yet none carried either a dinghy or even a life-preserver jacket, but all 12 returned safely in darkness, and Flt Lt Michael Peacock of 601 Squadron was awarded a DFC for his actions in this first RAF fighter foray against German territory.

For the first few weeks of the war Blenheims operated against enemy objectives from UK bases, though those under the aegis of No 2 Group, Bomber Command, were ostensibly on standby for possible transfer to France. At the outbreak of war 10 squadrons from No 1 Group — all Fairey Battles — had flown to France for short-range tactical

Below:
First RAF operational sortie in World War Two; Blenheim IV, N6215, of 139 Squadron, Wyton, on 3 September 1939. *Crown copyright*

Bottom:
First RAF awards. L-R: Flg Off A. McPherson, Flt Lt T. M. W. Smith, Flt Lt K. C. Doran, Flt Lt J. Barrett and Sgt W. E. Willitts after their investiture on 2 November 1939.

support for the British Expeditionary Force (BEF), but by mid-October it had been decided to re-equip some of Battle units with Blenheim IVs in England. Thus Nos 15 and 40 Squadrons serving with the Advanced Air Striking Force (AASF) in France were ordered back to England for refitment, 15 Squadron flying its Battles to Wyton on 9 and 10 December, followed there by 40 Squadron within days. To replace this pair of units on AASF strength, Nos 114 and 139 Squadrons received preliminary orders in early October for a move to France, and indeed three Blenheims of 114 Squadron were 'detached' to Villeneuve on 12 October to begin operations. Two of these flew their first sorties in France next day (N6232 and N6160), but the latter failed to return. In the event the final move of both units to the AASF came on 22 November.

While RAF units based along the so-termed 'Western Front' — a title recalling shades of the 1914-18 conflict — were kept mildly busy during the closing months of 1939, the onset of what proved to be the coldest winter in Europe for many decades further restricted aerial activities by all air forces in that zone. The same could not be said, however, for further north. Finland, an independent country for little more than 20 years, had been under considerable pressure for months prior to the war from its mammoth neighbour Russia to permit Soviet airfields and other military installations on Finnish territory, ostensibly for the 'defence' of the Leningrad area. With the signing of the Russo-German Non-Aggression Pact on 23 August 1939, Russia

felt free to 'expand', and on 17 September invaded Poland; then, on 30 November, she invaded Finland.

The ensuing war, known since as the 'Winter War', which erupted again in later years as the 'Continuation War' has received little attention from historians. Nevertheless, both conflicts emphasised the doughty qualities of the Bristol Blenheim I and IV, which were to become the most important bombers in the Finnish Air Forces for the next two decades. Dubbed *Pelti-Heikki*, the Blenheim was considered a pleasant design to fly by Finnish pilots, its chief handicap being inadequate defensive armament. No Finnish-built Blenheims had been completed before the 'Winter War' began, but in January 1940 12 Blenheim IVs (BL122-BL133) were flown from England via Stavanger, Norway by Finnish crews, one of which was lost in the North Sea on 18 January, and a second damaged in an accident and finally arriving in June. In February 1940 a further 12 Mk Is were delivered by RAF crews via Västeras to Juva (BL134-BL145). The Winter War lasted from November 1939 until March 1940, when the Finns were forced to accept an armistice with Russia and ceded a large area of Finnish territory to the Soviets. By then only 11 Blenheims were left in airworthy state of the initial English-built batches. During the remainder of 1940 the State Factory concentrated on repairing damaged Blenheims, but in

Below:
Blenheim IFs of 601 Squadron AAF, with nearest being piloted by Flt Lt Roger Bushell. *via J. R. Bushby*

Above:
Plt Off Whitney Straight and Blenheim IF, UF–B, of 601 Squadron AAF at Tangmere, 1940. *via RAF Museum*

Top right:
Blenheim Is of 92 Squadron, spring 1940.
via RAF Museum

Centre right:
Blenheim IV, N3627, LS–L of 15 Squadron, crashed at Wyton, 1940. Later, with 139 Squadron, it crashed on fire on 8 August 1941. *V. F. Bingham*

Bottom right:
Mk IV, XD–D of 139 Squadron in France, December 1939. *IWM*

1941 it began production of 15 Blenheim Is (BL146-BL160) and eventually produced further batches of Mk Is (BL161-BL190) in 1943, and 10 Mk IVs (BL196-BL205) in 1944. A small batch of Mk Is (BL191-BL195) were commenced but not completed. In June 1941, with the onslaught against Russia by Germany and its Allies, Russia began bombing operations along the Finnish frontier, and Finland immediately declared war by joining the Axis powers. At that moment the Finnish Air Force had three units equipped with Blenheims (a mixture of 24 Mk Is and three Mk IVs), which, with their later replacements, played a sturdy part in operations but suffered high casualties. Between June 1941 and the end of the Continuation War on 4 September 1944, when a final armistice with Russia brought an end to hostilities, a total of 47 Blenheims was lost, of which 29 were shot down or 'missing' in action, a further three destroyed on the ground and the remainder victims of 'accidents' — such as on 15 April 1942 when three were lost over their target when their bombs exploded prematurely.

Throughout both wars Finnish Blenheims had undertaken a wide variety of roles, operating as day-bombers, low level strikers, anti-submarine hunters and, particularly importantly, as photo-recce aircraft — this latter becoming one of the chief uses of the Finnish Blenheims in postwar years. The design had also been subject to several modifications to meet local operational requirements, including the use of fixed skis in place of wheels for winter work on many Mk Is during the Winter War. These skis — first tested in 1938 — were later modified to become retractable and were used in the early stages of the Continuation War. Initial Blenheim batches had been powered by 840hp Bristol Mercury VIII engines (later built in Finland under licence), but the main engines employed eventually were 920hp Mercury XVs. The longevity of Finnish Blenheims can be

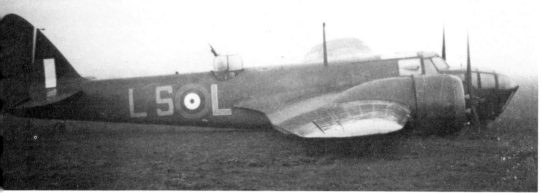

Above:
L8756, XD-E of 139 Squadron which later served as instructional machine and was SOC on 4 May 1944.
IWM

judged by their continuing use as trainers until ultimate retirement from service in 1957.

Throughout the arctic winter of 1939-40, while the Finnish Blenheim crews fought a desperate battle against vastly superior Russian odds, the Blenheim crews of the RAF further south saw relatively little action. In France Nos 114 and 139 Squadrons were serving under the aegis of the AASF by the close of 1939, while elsewhere along the Western Front as part of the BEF's Air Component were four other Blenheim IV units, Nos 18, 53, 57 and 59 Squadrons. All were basically employed on so-termed 'strategic reconnaissance' in support of the Allied Ground forces, undertaking mainly daylight photo-recce sorties over the battle zones and into Germany. The vulnerability of the Blenheim on such photo sorties soon became evident. In a total of 47 such sorties flown between 3 September and 31 December 1939, only 31 produced any photos, while eight Blenheims were 'lost', a figure representing a 17% loss rate of the total aircraft despatched. Plainly, the Blenheim lacked the necessary speed, range and defensive armament to operate efficiently or safely by day without heavy fighter escort. Some of these reconnaissances were undertaken by Blenheims of No 2 Group, Bomber Command from East Anglian bases in the UK, intermingled with that Group's main activities of North Sea anti-shipping patrols. The obviously inadequate armament of the Blenheim for daylight forays became an urgent matter for revision, and a variety of home-made ideas for under-tail and rearward-firing guns in engine nacelles were attempted in 2 Group squadrons at this period. A more practical solution was proposed by Wg Cdr Basil Embry, who suggested that the initial Bristol B1, Mk 1 mid-upper

gun turret with its single 0.303in calibre Lewis machine gun be replaced by a Mk IIIA turret mounting twin VGO 0.303in guns — a form of armament later to be replaced by twin 0.303in Brownings. Additionally it was proposed to install a gimbal-mounted hand-operated machine gun in the nose for the observer. Yet another urgent need incorporated, albeit tardily, was self-sealing fuel tanks.

At the start of 1940 No 2 Group had on strength seven Blenheim squadrons, Nos 15, 21, 40, 82, 101, 107 and 110, but of these Nos 15 and 40 were non-operational as yet, being in the process of re-equipping from Fairey Battles to Blenheim IVs. The five operational units then had as their prime role anti-shipping sorties of all forms; seeking out German merchant and Fleet vessels, keeping a constant watch on German harbours, ports and maritime movements, etc. Such operations meant flying mainly over the open sea in daylight without fighter escort, relying solely on tight formation self-defence when attacked by Luftwaffe fighters. Occasionally this form of defence proved worthwhile. On 10 January 1940 a formation of Blenheims from 110 Squadron, led by Sqn Ldr Kenneth Doran DFC, were attacked by five Messerschmitt Bf110s. Dropping down from 5,000ft to sea level, the Blenheims maintained a tight formation and by coolly co-ordinated shooting sent one Bf110 into the sea and damaged at least two others. Though several Blenheims sustained battle damage, the only loss was L4859 which fell out of formation with one engine

Above:
Blenheim IV, NT-J, believed of 29 OTU, with collapsed tail wheel.

Below:
Mk IV of 75 (Signals) Wing, 1941. *via RAF Museum*

47

Above:
First Finnish Air Force Blenheim, BL-104 on ski-undercarriage in 1938.

shattered and was shot down to explode into the sea. Doran was awarded a Bar to his DFC for his cool leadership, while nine awards of DFCs and DFMs went to other surviving crew members of this action. Throughout February 1940 No 2 Group's Blenheims could only mount operations on 10 days due directly to weather conditions; but in March the pace of operations increased considerably. On 11 March Sqn Ldr Miles Delap, piloting P4852, 'O' of 82 Squadron, accomplished an historic 'first' when he surprised a surfaced German U-boat, *U31*, and sank it with his four 250lb GP bombs — the first U-boat 'kill' by an unaided RAF aircraft in World War 2.*

In April and early May 1940 No 2 Group's Blenheims continued their anti-shipping roles over the North Sea, though with relatively little success to show for their efforts, but by then Allied fears of a forthcoming spring offensive by German forces had led to orders being issued to most UK-based bomber squadrons detailing possible future objectives in Holland, Belgium and northern France should such an offensive materialise; a possibility very much enhanced by German invasions of Norway and Denmark at that time. No 2 Group's Blenheim squadrons were initially earmarked to move to France for support of the BEF, but lack of French air-fields to accommodate them delayed, then cancelled, this intention by the close of 1939. Instead the units were to remain based in England, under Bomber Command control but ready to 'assist' the AASF and Air Component, BEF when 'requested' by Air Marshal Arthur Barratt, AOC RAF in France. Their future role was projected as low level ground attack against enemy troop and vehicle movements, apart from a slightly vague 'reconnoitring' watch-and-ward responsibility. Such operations would necessarily be flown mainly by day without properly organised fighter escort — a daunting prospect for the

Blenheim crews, particularly at virtual zero altitude with all the incumbent risks of flak and natural terrain hazards. Then, on 10 May 1940, even as further orders outlining possible tactics and objectives continued to reach Blenheim squadrons, German forces launched their massive triple-pronged blitzkrieg assaults against the Low Countries and France. In the succinct summing up of one veteran Blenheim skipper, 'Suddenly the war became bloody dangerous'.

The parts played by the UK-based and French-based Blenheim squadrons in attempting to stem the German 'steamroller' advances were determined, gallant and relatively brief; plunging into battle against hopeless odds in piecemeal fashion, and suffering grim casualty rates. On 10 May 1940 the Blenheim units in England and France were disposed as follows:

Squadron	Base
15	Alconbury (satellite to unit base at Wyton)
18	Meharicourt
21	Bodney
40	Wyton
53	Poix
57	Rosières-en-Santerre
59	Poix
82	Watton
101	West Raynham
107	Wattisham
110	Wattisham
114	Condé Vraux
139	Plivot

U31, which on that date was on sea trials following a refit, was salvaged by the Germans, eventually re-entered active service but was sunk by HMS *Antelope* in November 1940.

Above and overleaf:
**Views of Finnish Air Force Blenheim Is during the
'Winter War'.** *Cinema video des Armees, Paris*

Between them these held an overall total of some 230
Blenheim IVs on that date, 108 of these in France.
Allied intelligence had indicated a distinct possibility
of such a German advance from as early as January
1940, thus all Blenheim squadrons (among others)
had in essence been at some stage of standby
'readiness' for weeks before the actual assaults; yet
the German moves still came unexpectedly in the
contexts of strength, direction and speed. As each

unit received news of the advances early on 10 May,
all crews were put on immediate readiness.

Despite the various dawn attacks on Allied airfields in France by the Luftwaffe, the Blenheim
squadrons suffered little damage on 10 May, and
most units began despatching single or pairs of aircraft to seek out the forward German troop movements. At 09.00hrs, for example, two Blenheims of
15 Squadron reconnoitred the Dutch and Belgian
border bridges for signs of German forces, both
returning safely to base by 13.00hrs; while five
minutes after this pair took off two aircraft of 40
Squadron were leaving base to scout the Hague area,
one of which failed to return. By noon reports of
strong German paratroop invasions of Belgian and

Dutch strongpoints and airfields were coming into Allied headquarters, and various formations of Blenheims assembled to attack these threats. Shortly after 14.00hrs eight Blenheims of 15 Squadron left to bomb the Waalhaven airport of Rotterdam, all returning scathed by flak but intact; but a second formation of 12 Blenheims of 40 Squadron despatched to bomb Ypenburg lost two aircraft to the fierce defences. At 16.50hrs 12 Blenheims of 110 Squadron joined with six Mk IFs of 600 Squadron for a low level bombing and strafing raid on a gaggle of Junkers Ju52 troop carriers reported on a beach north of the Hague. Braving an inferno of ground fire, and attacked by a dozen Messerschmitt Bf110s, the Blenheim IFs destroyed several Junkers but were heavily scarred; only one aircraft actually landing back at base, while one Mk IF, piloted by Plt Off R. Haine, force-landed in Holland and its crew joined the complement of personnel, including the Dutch royal family, aboard a destroyer bound for England. Six more IFs of 600 Squadron later attacked opportunity targets in the Middlekerck-Zeebrugge-Flushing areas, destroying a Heinkel bomber on the ground, and all returned safely. As a result of these two actions three DFCs and one DFM award went to participating members of 600 Squadron. The day was rounded out by further reconnaissance sorties by various Blenheims. Throughout that first day of the blitzkrieg assault at

least 13 Blenheims had been lost or destroyed, while many others bore ready evidence of the accuracy of the mobile German 88mm flak guns on the ground.

At first light on 11 May nine Dornier Do17Zs of II/KG2 from Aschaffenburg base hugged the terrain as they swept westwards, heading specifically for an Allied airfield at Conde Vraux, near Sissonne-La Malmaison. Achieving total surprise, the Dornier crews reached their objective and found the full complement of 114 Squadron's Blenheims lined up wing to wing, fully armed and fuelled and about to leave for a raid in the Maastricht area. Flying along the line of Blenheims, the Dornier crews released accurate sticks of 100lb bombs, made one full circuit of the airfield, then made a second equally accurate bomb-run. The lack of Allied opposition in any form gave the last Dornier crew leisure to film the results with a cine-camera — a line of burning, exploding Blenheims and other aircraft amounting to some 30 observed on fire. In mere minutes, 114 Squadron had been to all intents decimated. Several days later this cine-film was being viewed by the German Führer, Adolf Hitler.

Elsewhere, other assaults on Allied airfields produced a crop of aircraft losses on the ground, but UK-based Blenheim units at immediate readiness for bombing raids in France were delayed from taking off until the mid-afternoon. Just before 15.00hrs 11 aircraft of 110 Squadron, followed shortly after by 11 Blenheims of 21 Squadron, left bases to attack enemy troops occupying various bridges across the Maas. They were met by a holocaust of flak and wheeling German fighters, and each squadron lost two aircraft; while other Blenheim units on similar sorties lost at least five more, and the survivors returned to base bearing gaping scars and wounded

Top:
Blenheim Boys. Personnel of 18 Squadron, France, winter 1939-40. OC Sqn, Wg Cdr Opie is centre-front.

Above:
Blenheim IV, L9191, an 18 Squadron aircraft, crashed at Crecy, 19 May 1940.

Right:
Blenheim IF, L8679, BQ-D of 600 Squadron AAF which was damaged by 'friendly' anti-aircraft gunfire on 9 August 1940 and abandoned in the air.

Top right:
82 Squadron Mk IVs at Watton, early 1940. Nearest, P6915, UX-A was lost on 7 June 1940. *via RAF Museum*

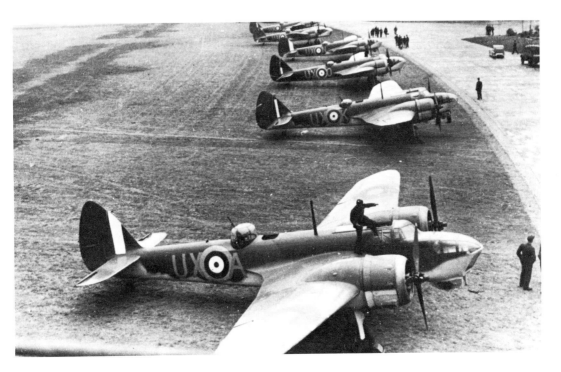

crew men. The battle for the Maas bridges continued on 12 May, despite increased flak defences and the ever-present attentions of Messerschmitt Bf109Es of the crack *Jagdgeschwader* JG27, commanded by Max Ibel. From virtual dawn to dusk the RAF and French bombers attempted to penetrate such fierce defences — and suffered accordingly. At 08.10hrs, led by the dynamic Wg Cdr Basil Embry, a dozen Blenheims of 107 Squadron tried to bomb the Maas bridges and lost four crews in the trying, to flak and fighters. An hour later 12 Blenheims of 15 Squadron also tried, lost six crews and could only repair two of the surviving machines; in effect, the squadron had been wiped out for the moment in terms of operational use. Eleven Blenheims of 110 Squadron were in a similar raid that day and lost two; but further sorties in the early evening by 82 and 21 Squadrons escaped losses, except for L8739 of 21 Squadron which had its rear fuselage blown away over Tongres. Total Blenheim losses for 12 May reached at least 19, including seven (of nine) Blenheims of 139 Squadron shot down by Messerschmitt Bf109Es of JG27 over Maastricht.

In view of the mounting bomber casualties, RAF operations on 13 May were officially stopped, yet even then three aircraft of 59 Squadron (L9266, N6173 P6926) and one from 57 Squadron (P6930) are recorded as 'Missing in action'. On 14 May, however, an all-out effort was made to stem a German breakthrough in the Sedan area, and the day was soon to become a maelstrom of clashes between the Luftwaffe fighters and British and French aerial formations lasting most of the day with little pause. RAF losses for the day escalated swiftly to a grim tally of at least 40 Battles and Blenheims shot out of the sky from a total of 71 despatched — a casualty *percentage* never exceeded in RAF operations of any comparison throughout the entire war. Next day at least seven more Blenheims were lost in action, including P4913 of 40 Squadron which was shot down by an RAF Hurricane, and L9399 of 53 Squadron, also a victim of poor identification by another Hurricane pilot! Tragic as such casualties were, they were surpassed on 17 May when 12 Blenheims of 82 Squadron from Watton tried to bomb a German armoured formation on the Gembloux-Namur road at approximately 07.00hrs. Flak and (mainly) Bf109Es massacred the bombers within minutes, and only one Blenheim (L8858, 'W') scraped home to Watton — and even this machine disintegrated at the end of its landing run, so severe was its battle damage. Elsewhere that day 15 Squadron had three of a six-Blenheim formation shot down, with two of the remaining three so badly shot up that they were declared beyond worthwhile repair.

The saga of disaster — and indomitable courage — was to continue throughout the month of May 1940. Casualty figures mounted in horrific leaps and bounds among the RAF bomber units — in the nine days up to 22 May on which No 2 Group Blenheims operated, 44 aircraft were lost and more than 100 aircrew members killed — and by the end of the month the overall Blenheim losses had totted up to *at least* 150 aircraft — the rough equivalent of nearly

Top:
Blenheim IV, RT-L of 114 Squadron abandoned at Conde Vraux, France, 1940.

Above:
K7064, SY-H of 139 Squadron.

nine fully established Blenheim squadrons. Such statistics do not account for dozens of other aircraft which 'survived' actual sorties but were hardly worth repairing, such was their battle damage. The most tragic aspect, however, was the irreplaceable loss of so many experienced aircrewmen, most of whom were prewar-trained professionals, and many of whom had been flight or squadron commanders. Replacement crews from the slowly burgeoning RAF and Empire training schemes had yet to take their places in the frontline units. Yet in spite of such daunting losses, decimated squadrons were quickly replenished and returned to operations, even more determined to pursue their duties; perhaps the most obvious example being the massacred 82 Squadron

which, due mainly to drive of Wg Cdr the Earl of Bandon, resumed operations on 20 May, just three days after its greatest defeat. Just three months later, on 13 August, 82 Squadron was to suffer a second massive defeat, when 11 of a 12-Blenheim formation despatched to bomb Aalborg airfield were lost, five to flak and a further six to the guns of JG77's Messerschmitt Bf109Es...

From 26 May to 4 June Operation 'Dynamo' was in force — the seaborne evacuation of Allied armies from the beaches of Dunkirk — and Blenheim crews continued their daily offensive against German targets in Europe. Even when 'Dynamo' ceased, Allied troops in France continued their opposition to advancing German forces, and most bomber operations were aimed at supporting the remaining Allied resistance. Such sorties inevitably incurred further losses to flak and enemy fighters, despite occasional help from escorting RAF fighters. Then, on 22 June, the French government finally agreed to an armistice with Germany; the French debacle was over.

6
Night Hunters

Mention has been made (see chapter 2) of the pioneering part played by the Blenheim If in the initial development of Airborne Interception (AI) radar in the context of night interception roles. The original selection of the Blenheim for the early trials of AI resulted from the contemporary AOC-in-C Fighter Command's recommendation that a twin-engined, multi-crewed aircraft be employed, rather than the conventional single-seat fighter. At that time (1939) the Blenheim IF fitted such requirements admirably — at least, in theory — and, in any case, was really the only such design readily available in RAF use then. This was not to say, however, that it was ideal for such a purpose. The overall weight of the earliest AI installations — close to 600lb — in a Mk IF had only minor effect on the aircraft's performance, but the bulky 'black boxes' and their associated paraphernalia, which initially had not been designed specifically for aerial carriage, tended to take up a large proportion of an already cramped fuselage interior. Up front the pilot was virtually surrounded by flat Perspex panels. By day these provided excellent all-round vision for him, but by night they tended to reflect and distort all light sources from inside and outside the aircraft. Behind him, facing aft, the set operator had his hands full attempting to cope with the vagaries of the AI installation — these ranging from an abhorrence of

even mildly damp atmospheres, to overheating and emitting smoke, or, too often, complete non-functioning. In these circumstances it became necessary to carry a third crew member simply to attend to the guns and ammunition feed.

Even if all went well with the radar, there were many other problems to be overcome before any possibility of a successful interception by night. The radar sets were not only unreliable but often ambiguous in what they displayed, and seldom precise enough to guarantee any interception, while any incoming raider deliberately keeping well below 7,500ft altitude could not even be suspected on the fighter's visual screen. The multitude of variables and technical troubles meant that the earliest Blenheim AI crews spent long, frustrating hours searching the raven blackness of night without (usually) ever actually making a contact. Nevertheless, AI offered the only real future for night interception of the Luftwaffe and the crews persevered. In November 1939 three AI-equipped machines were delivered to a detached flight of No 600 Squadron AAF based at Manston for crew-training, under the command of Sqn Ldr (later, Air Marshal, Sir) Walter Pretty. On 11 March 1940, Flg Off (later, Sqn Ldr) A. H. H. Tollemache was about to land at Manston after a searchlight co-operation sortie when his Blenheim struck a tree near the flarepath, crashed in a nearby field, and erupted in flames. Tollemache and his LAC gunner struggled free uninjured, but an army lieutenant passenger remained trapped in the burning wreckage. In spite of the flames and exploding ammunition, Tollemache made valiant efforts to

Below:
Blenheim IF, YB-L of 29 Squadron at Debden prior to the war. *BAe*

Above:
Mk IF convert with belly gun pack (minus guns here).

Below:
604 Squadron AAF on parade at Northolt, April 1940, being inspected by newly-appointed Secretary of State for Air, Sir Samuel Hoare. OC Sqn was Sqn Ldr M. F. Anderson.

Below:
23 Squadron Mk IF, YP-Q at Wittering, January 1940.
MoD (Air)

Bottom:
**Night Owls. Crew of 29 Squadron mount their steed for
a night patrol.** *IWM*

Above:
Black Beauty. Z5722, WM-Z of 68 Squadron, personal aircraft of the OC Sqn, Wg Cdr Hon Max Aitken DFC, in all-black livery. *via RAF Museum*

rescue the man, but was finally forced away with his clothing alight. His burns were treated at Archie McIndoe's East Grinstead 'Guinea Pigs' hospital, and on 6 August 1940 Tollemache was awarded an Empire Gallantry Medal, an award second only in precedence to the Victoria Cross*.

No 600 Squadron's Blenheim Flight became the nucleus of six AI-equipped Blenheims which formed a new unit, the Fighter Interception Unit (FIU), on 10 April 1940 at Tangmere, commanded by Wg Cdr (later, Air Marshal, Sir) G. P. Chamberlain. These Blenheims were fitted with Mk II, then Mk III AI radar sets, but results were still elusive. The lengthy lack of positive success with the 'Magic Mirrors' — the aircrews' name for the radar installations — ended abruptly, albeit momentarily, on the night of 22/23 July 1940. That night Flg Off G. Ashfield, with his crew of Plt Off G. E. Morris and Sgt R. H. Leyland (set operator), in an FIU Blenheim fitted with a Mk IV AI, were skilfully 'talked' on to an incoming Dornier Do17 of 2/.KG3 and shot it down into the Channel — the first-ever successful RAF night interception by airborne radar. It was, nevertheless, the first bright spot in an otherwise gloomy picture to date. Further 'one-off' successes slowly followed. A Heinkel He111 of KG53 was shot down in the early hours of 18 August by a 29 Squadron crew, the first of three claims that month by that squadron; on 3/4 September Plt Off Herrick of 25 Squadron claimed two victims, followed by a third later in the month; while on the night of 15/16 September No 600 Squadron claimed its first

confirmed night victim when Flt Lt C. A. Pritchard destroyed a Junkers Ju88 (the unit records said a Heinkel). Heartening as such victories were to by the patient Blenheim crews, they were but isolated instances, as exemplified on the night of 14/15 November 1940 when more than 400 Luftwaffe bombers devastated the cathedral city of Coventry. Of the 129 individual fighter interception sorties flown that night, 39 were by Blenheim crews. Of the latter only two actually fired their guns, but none achieved a victory.

Five nights after the Coventry raid another AI 'kill' was registered, but on this occasion by a Beaufighter, R2098 of No 604 Squadron, piloted by Flt Lt (later, Gp Capt) John Cunningham. A 'junior' stablemate of the Blenheim, the Beaufighter had first entered FIU service on 12 August 1940, and the type flew its first night sortie (R2059) with the unit on 4/5 September 1940. With its advantages of greater speed and much heavier armament, the Beaufighter then steadily replaced the Blenheim in night-fighter units throughout the winter of 1940-41. The transition from Blenheims to Beaufighters was spread over several months, however, and when No 68 Squadron was reformed at Catterick as a night-fighter unit on 7 January 1941 it was initially given Blenheim IFs and a few Mk IVFs. In April 1941, commanded by Wg Cdr Hon Max Aitken DFC, 68 Squadron moved to High Ercall and commenced operations with Blenheims, but in the following month began to receive its first Beaufighters. By then most other night-fighter squadrons had also exchanged their Blenheims for Beaufighters, and the night-hunting Blenheim faded from the 'sharp end' operational scene. Though able to show few 'kills' for all their long hours of night-stalking, the Blenheims had pioneered the radar-guided night-fighting techniques of the RAF over a period of some two years, and set the scene for future escalating success by their inheritor Beaufighter and Mosquito crews in later years.

*Tollemache's EGM was exchanged for a George Cross when this award was instituted on 24 September 1940.

7
'Circus' and 'Roadstead'

The cruel lessons of the 1940 French debacle had unquestionably highlighted the extreme vulnerability of unescorted light and medium bombers undertaking day operations, witnessed by the charred wrecks of hundreds of Battles, Blenheims and other Allied aircraft strewn on the plains and forestland of Flanders and the Sedan at the close of that tragic conflict. Remembering too the similar RAF losses on such sorties in late 1939, it may be wondered why the RAF hierarchy continued to despatch Blenheims

on daylight operations thereafter. In truth, RAF commanders had little alternative in 1940-41 if indeed the overall policy of a constant aerial offensive (as opposed to pure defensive) was to be maintained at that period. Though Bomber Command's Whitleys, Wellingtons, and Hampdens maintained a steady night war against German targets, the Blenheim IV was the only *available* bomber on the squadrons even capable of mounting any form of day operations over Occupied Europe in any strength. Even so, any possibility of provision of adequate fighter escorting 'umbrella' in the summer

Below:
Sweep. Blenheim IVFs of 254 Squadron setting out on a coastal anti-shipping patrol, mid-1941. *PNA*

Bottom:
Blenheim IVs of 21 Squadron (nearest, V5595, YH-P) run in fast and low towards Rotterdam on 16 July 1941. V5595 had previously served with 101 Squadron. *British Official*

Above:
Crews of 114 Squadron on 13 February 1942, the morning after the 'Channel Dash' operations against the German capital ships *Scharnhorst, Gneisenau* and *Prinz Eugen*. In greatcoat, Earl of Bandon. Of 48 Blenheim sorties despatched, 36 aborted, two were lost to enemy aircraft, with a third severely damaged.

Below:
Blenheim IV of 40 Squadron with under-nose, rearward-firing single Browning gun.

Below right:
Mk IVFs of 235 Squadron at Bircham Newton, circa late 1940. *via RAF Museum*

and autumn of 1940 was obviated by Fighter Command's total absorption with defending the United Kingdom from Luftwaffe assault in the Battle of Britain. Moreover, the early marks of Hurricane and Spitfire in firstline use in 1940 were incapable of providing worthwhile long range protection.

Evidence of the odds against day bombers came from the casualty rates and was amply illustrated by comparison with the losses of nightbombers during the period 9/10 May to 4/5 June 1940. Nightraiders from Nos 3, 4, and 5 Groups, Bomber Command flew a total of 1,696 sorties and lost 39 aircraft but Blenheims of No 2 Group, operating by day, lost 56 in 856 sorties, apart from many others damaged beyond repair. Nevertheless, the crucial need to assist Fighter Command's desperate struggle with the Luftwaffe over southern England after France's capitulation in 1940 brought the Blenheim squadrons into battle yet again by day. Their prime role was to attack directly any build-up of German invasion barges and other vessels in any Channel ports, but of equal importance was a policy from early June 1940 to raid Luftwaffe airfields in France and the Low Countries, thereby (hopefully) to 'pin down' the German fighters and bombers. The latter hope was, at best, optimistic; at that time the Luftwaffe occupied some 400 airfields from which it could launch attacks against England, a total which would have stretched the whole capacity of Bomber Command, let alone the handful of Blenheim units. Inevitably, the onus of responsibility for such sorties fell almost wholly upon the battered shoulders of No 2 Group's Blenheim squadrons. The only sop to 'protection' for the Blenheim day-raiders was an instruction from Group HQ that all such sorties were to be pursued '... only when cloud cover gives adequate security' — and order which was translated to mean that any sortie having less than 7/10s cloud cover must be abandoned. The first such 2 Group attack was flown by Blenheims of Nos 15, 18 and 82 Squadrons against Boos airfield on 19 June; followed later in the day by more attacks on Amiens/Glisy. It was the start for 2 Group's Blenheim crews of a virtual nine-month campaign against Luftwaffe bases.

The naked dangers of such sorties can best be illustrated by such raids as those undertaken by 2 Group Blenheims on 9 and 10 July. On 9 July six crews of 21 Squadron joined with six more from 57 Squadron in attacking Stavanger airfield in Norway. Flak and fighters shot down four of 21 Squadron, two of 57 Squadron, sent Wg Cdr L. C. Bennett down to ditch in the sea and left the five surviving aircraft heavily damaged. Next day 107 Squadron despatched six Blenheims to bomb an airfield near Amiens — only one crew returned. July 1940 saw 2 Group with a strength of 11 squadrons — some 180 operational aircraft — but losses in that month totalled 31 in action (including three wing commanders killed), apart from seven other aircraft written off to damage or crashes. The following month, August, added a further 28 Blenheims lost in action, 10 more wrecked and the loss of 60 aircrewmen. Not all such sorties had been by day, however. The Blenheim IV's fighting range allowed modest penetration beyond the German borders, and 2 Group initiated a sporadic series of night 'intruder' and night bombing raids from July 1940. September 1940 proved to be 2 Group's busiest month to date, with slightly more than 500 individual sorties being

flown, while losses amounted to 19 'missing' and six
others written off charge due to severe damage.
Throughout those fateful months — the peak of the
Battle of Britain it should be remembered — the
Blenheim crews had ample 'practice' in attacking a
fairly wide variety of objectives; tackling airfields,
ports, heavy gun positions, oil installations, barge
concentrations and enemy shipping, as well as more
general North Sea sweeps and reconnaissances. By
November however the main emphasis became
'intruder' attacks by night against firstline Luftwaffe
airfields, in support of main bombing raids.

The main concentration of night-raiding for 2
Group's Blenheims continued through the winter
months of 1940-41, but on 10 January 1941 a fresh
tactic was instigated. On that date a single Blenheim
squadron (No 114), escorted by no less than nine
fighter squadrons, crossed the French coast heading
for an airfield near Pas de Calais. Its purpose was
basically to 'suck up' Luftwaffe fighter opposition,
though on this occasion only two Messerschmitt
Bf109s were met, both of which were shot down by
the fighter escort led by Wg Cdr F. V. Beamish
DSO, AFC. It was effectively the first of a continuing series of similar operations with the same
basic purpose, ie blatant attempts to draw the
German fighters up into a battle of fighter attrition,
using the Blenheims as 'bait'. This type of operation
was code-named 'Circus', and unfavourable weather
delayed the second such foray until 2 February,
when six Blenheims of 139 Squadron, escorted by
Hurricanes of 601 Squadron AAF, raided the
Boulogne docks and returned without losses. During
the remaining months of 1941 the size and specific
aims of 'Circus' operations increased and varied in
numbers and scope respectively, with as many as 24

Above:
V5468, 'O' of 114 Squadron at West Raynham, early 1942. This machine took part in the first '1,000-bomber raid' on Cologne on night of 30/31 May 1942.

Above right:
21 Squadron Mk IV on return to Chivenor after an operation, circa April 1941, displaying extensive nose damage. *via RAF Museum*

Below:
V6240, YH-B of 21 Squadron, which failed to return on 12 July 1941. *Central Press*

or more Blenheims, in 'boxes' of six, being escorted by — on occasion — hundreds of fighters. Such sorties involved complex and intricate planning, yet the first six months of these produced relatively poor 'profits' in terms of enemy aircraft *actually* destroyed. This can be illustrated by the RAF fighter costs and claims. In just six weeks in June-July 1941, in 46 'Circus' operations, the RAF lost 123 fighter pilots, but claimed destruction of 322 German fighters — a figure greater than the entire German fighter strength in the west at that period. Indeed, RAF fighter pilots claimed a total of 731 German aircraft destroyed from mid-June until the end of 1941, with RAF fighter losses totalling 426. The *actual* German loss figure for this period was merely 103 aircraft destroyed. The relatively small Luftwaffe fighter strength opposing the 1941 'Circus' (and other) day sorties was due simply to dilution in the early months of the year by steady transfer to the east, as Hitler prepared for his sudden invasion of Russia. Despite numerical inferiority — the lowest numerical level of fighter strength since the outbreak of the war — the German defenders were led by veteran commanders, such as Adolf Galland, while the improved Messerschmitt Bf109F entered squadron service in mid-1941, followed in August by the Focke Wulf Fw190; the latter fresh design establishing itself as superior to any contemporary RAF fighter in squadron use.

From March 1941, stemming from a directive from the Prime Minister, Winston Churchill, Fighter, Bomber and Coastal Commands began concerting some of their individual efforts towards nullifying the mounting losses of Allied merchant shipping to German U-boats and surface raiders, at the same time intensifying assaults on enemy harbours, ports, U-boats bases and — particularly — Axis merchant shipping in European coastal waters in a bid to blockade Germany's seaborne supplies of vital materials. Though promulgated as 'top priority' then by Churchill, anti-shipping operations by Blenheim crews were hardly an innovation. From early 1940 Blenheim squadrons had been serving under the aegis of Coastal Command, patrolling and scouring European waters, apart from providing medium-range protection escort to Allied convoys. These units were:

Squadron	Remarks
53	Transferred to Coastal Command (C/Cmd) July 1940
59	Transferred to C/Cmd July 1940
86	Formed Gosport 6/12/40; began ops 28/3/41
143	Formed Aldergrove 15/6/41
235	Transferred C/Cmd Feb 1940; began ops May 1940
236	Transferred C/Cmd Feb 1940; began ops June 1940
248	Transferred C/Cmd Feb 1940; began ops June 1940
252	Reformed Bircham Newton, C/Cmd, 21/11/40
254	Transferred C/Cmd Jan 1940; began ops Feb 1940
272	Formed 19/11/40, C/Cmd; began ops Feb 1941
404 RCAF	Formed Thorney Island 15/4/41; began ops Sep 1941
500 AAF	Operated Blenheims 8/4/41 to Dec 1941, C/Cmd
608 AAF	Operated Blenheims 2/2/41 to July 1941 C/Cmd

All flew Blenheim IVs, mainly IVFs with the additional gun packs, having in many cases been previously employed with Fighter Command.

Known collectively by the generic code-name 'Roadstead', this latest concentration and anti-shipping strikes by Bomber Command's Blenheims quickly emphasised the great hazards of such operations. Of necessity such attacks had to be pressed home at virtual shipmast-height in the teeth of ferocious flak opposition, apart from the added dangers from any Luftwaffe fighter escorts, and required an especially high degree of determination and courage on the part of Blenheim skippers. The brunt of such Blenheim sorties was undertaken by the crews of No 2 Group — and they suffered grievously. From mid-March until late November 1941 the Blenheim squadrons of No 2 Group remained committed to 'Roadstead' operations as top priority, though other concomitant types of equally hazardous operations were added to their responsibility; one such being 'Channel Stop', which from April 1941 was an outright attempt by the RAF in southeast England to 'close off' the Dover end of the English Channel to enemy shipping by day. Such sorties usually took the form of a small section of Blenheims — often only three aircraft — being heavily escorted by Spitfires and Hurricanes from a forward airfield (Manston primarily) in sea level strikes against enemy ships sighted, the fighters acting as spearhead to smother flak opposition as well as top cover from Luftwaffe interference. Blenheim casualties were high indeed; some units employed on 'Channel Stop' lasted no longer than two weeks before it proved necessary to withdraw them from operations for aircraft and personnel replacement to bring the unit up to fighting strength again.

A glance at the Blenheim casualty statistics relating to these anti-shipping operations illustrates vividly the toll incurred. From mid-March to mid-April 1941, the first month of this 'campaign', nine Blenheims were lost, and many others returned with battle scars and wounded or dead crew members. It was a relatively mild start to an escalating casualty rate during subsequent months. The three months April to June 1941 saw 36 Blenheims lost in action, representing some 12% of total aircraft despatched on sorties; but in the month of August alone this rate rose to some 30% when 23 of a total of 77 despatched failed to return, apart from 13 others lost on other forms of day operations. Such figures must

Above:
Back from an op.

be set against the 2 Group strength of available Blenheims for operations, which averaged no more than 120-140 during the first eight months of that year, and do not include the casualties incurred by those Blenheims from the Group which commenced detachments to Malta for anti-shipping operations in the Mediterranean theatre from June 1941.

No matter which specific type of operation undertaken by the Blenheim crews of 2 Group throughout 1941, one common denominator for all was ultra-low level flying; a Group 'penchant' particularly exemplified on 12 August when a total of 54 Blenheims from Nos 18, 21, 82, 107, 114, 139 and 226 Squadrons set out to attack two targets in Germany, the Goldenberg power plant at Knapsack and Fortuna plant at Quadrath, both near Cologne. Each Blenheim carried two 500lb GP/HE bombs, and the bombing force was heavily escorted and protected by many hundreds of fighters, directly or indirectly. Flying no higher than 100ft throughout the entire outward flight, the Blenheims achieved a modicum of surprise and duly bombed their respective targets despite fierce flak opposition. Attacks

from Luftwaffe fighters were, in the main, thwarted by the RAF fighter cover, but 12 Blenheims failed to return from this twin attack, the deepest penetration raid by day into Germany to date. On 28 August a force of 18 Blenheims from Nos 21, 88, 110 and 226 Squadrons, escorted by two Spitfire squadrons, attacked shipping at Rotterdam. Of these 12 were lost to flak, fighters and crashes. The daylight sorties continued throughout the remaining months of 1941, albeit on a diminishing frequency due to unfavourable weather, and the last 2 Group raid of the year was mounted on 27 December — a combined Services' assault against Vaagso and other nearby objectives in Norway. Thirteen Blenheims from 114 Squadron and six from 110 Squadron participated, losing five in all. Overall, 1941 had been a year of intense and costly operations for the UK-based Blenheim squadrons; a prolonged period of high sacrifice and great courage for their crews. By late October Blenheims had finally been withdrawn from the 'Roadstead' operations, due to their obvious unsuitability for such sorties; while postwar enemy records revealed that the overall achievement of this type of anti-shipping offensive had resulted in just 29 ships being sunk and 21 others seriously damaged, a total less than one-third of even the most cautious contemporary Allied claims.

In the context of the European air war at the close

Above:
**Mk IVs of 21 Squadron at Chivenor on 4 April 1941,
mainly painted black on all undersurfaces.**
via RAF Museum

of 1941, the increasing unsuitability of the Blenheim IV for bombing operations was well recognised, both by 'higher authority' and — especially — the crews. The design's most obvious inadequacies were insufficient speed, defensive armament and bombload, none of which could be significantly improved by any form of modification without having an adverse effect on the other failings. Like its fellow prewar designs, Wellington, Whitley and Hampden, the Blenheim had helped to 'hold the fort' in Bomber Command during the desperate years 1939-41, patiently awaiting replacement by promised

four-engined 'heavies' like the Stirling and Halifax, and (eventually) Lancaster. By December 1941 all three of these latter had begun to enter squadron use, while better-performance twin-engined bombers like the American Douglas Boston were available to commence replacing the battle-weary Blenheim in firstline service as medium range strike aircraft. The steady decline in operational use is reflected in Bomber Command's strength statistics for 9 January 1942, when an overall total of 96 Blenheim IVs was spread thinly between eight squadrons; yet on 23 February only three squadrons were still operating the type, having a gross total of 51 aircraft available. In the event Blenheims continued to be used by Bomber Command until August 1942; their ultimate sorties being night-intruder probes against some Dutch and German airfields on the night of 17/18 August by Blenheims of No 18 Squadron; the final Blenheim, Z7295, 'F' of 18 Squadron, landing back at base at 01.45hrs on 18 August.

8
Around the Med

The RAF's Middle East Command by 1939 was a deceptively simple title for a vast area of RAF responsibilities, encompassing 'air control' duties in Egypt, Sudan, Palestine, Trans-Jordan, Iraq, Aden, East Africa, Somaliland, the oil-rich Persian Gulf, Balkan border areas, Malta and the Mediterranean zone generally — in a geographical context, an area in toto greater than the land mass of the USA. To fulfil its many wide-ranging responsibilities 'Around the Med', the RAF at the outbreak of World War 2 had to rely on a motley array of (mainly) obsolescent, even obsolete, aircraft designs spread thinly throughout the command; a majority of which were outmoded biplanes. Nevertheless, the obvious necessity for 'modernising' equipment of the Middle East squadrons had been appreciated by the Air Ministry prior to the war, and among the thin trickle of up-dated aircraft types slowly to be introduced in the Middle East was the Blenheim I bomber; the first example arriving on No 30 Squadron at Dhibban*, Iraq on 13 January 1938.

Between that date and 10 June 1940 — when the Italian dictator Mussolini formally declared war against the Allies — more Blenheims arrived in the Middle East to replace outdated aircraft, and on the day Italy entered the conflict the following Blenheim units were ready for operations:

*Renamed Habbaniyah on 25 March 1938.

Squadron	Base	No of Blenheims
8	Khormaksar, Aden	12 (+6 Vincents)
11	Sheik Othman, Aden	9
30	Ismailia, Egypt	12
39	Sheik Othman, Aden	9
45	Fuka, Egypt	12
55	Fuka, Egypt	12
84	Shaibah, Iraq	12
113	Ma-aten Bagush, Egypt	12
211	Daba, Egypt	12

This total of 102 operationally-ready Blenheims was supported by merely three other pure bomber squadrons, Nos 14, 47 and 223, all flying Vickers Wellesleys; though No 70 Squadron (Vickers Valentias) and 216 Squadron (Bristol Bombays) were technically titled as 'Bomber-Transport' units. Of the nine Blenheim squadrons, almost all were operating Mk I bombers, though 113 Squadron, which had re-equipped with Mk Is in June-September 1939, began receiving Mk IVs from March 1940. Another 'mixed' unit was No 30 Squadron which, in June 1940, 'converted' its B and C Flights' Mk Is to Mk IF 'fighter' standards by locally fitting four-gun belly packs, leaving its A Flight as Mk I bombers.

In the early dawn of 11 June 1940 the RAF in Egypt struck its first blow against an Italian target, when 26 Blenheims drawn from Nos 45, 55 and 113 Squadrons strafed and bombed the Italian airfield at

Below:
K7097 of 30 Squadron, 1938 ('P'), which crashed near Habbaniyah, Iraq on 10 December 1938.

El Adem. Flak and fighter opposition was relatively fierce, claiming two Blenheims and forcing a third to crash-land at Sidi Barrani. This example of a policy of attack being the best form of defence inaugurated a continuing offensive role by all RAF units in the Middle East, with the Blenheim squadrons well to the fore on most occasions. The Blenheim force was slightly depleted from July 1940 when 45 Squadron detached its A Flight to Erkowit in the Sudan, but on 26 September reinforcements in the shape of four Blenheims arrived in the command; they were the first such to arrive in Egypt since the collapse of France, and had been ferried in from Takoradi, West Africa. This trans-Sahara route was to become the main source of future aircraft reinforcement for Middle East Command.

In the summer and autumn of 1940 the Blenheim operations against Italian objectives steadily increased in strength, often comprising four or five squadrons combining their efforts, with a fighter escort to ward off air opposition. In October, however, the overall tactical situation in the Mediterranean theatre changed abruptly when Italy invaded Greece from Albania. A British offer of immediate aid with forces was, for the moment, declined by the Greek government, with the exception of aerial support. Accordingly, No 30 Squadron flew its Blenheims to Eleusis on 1 November to help defend Athens, and began 'reconverting' some of its Mk IFs back to Mk I bomber status. In the event, 30 Squadron was to revert to full fighter role, and by 3 March 1941 was henceforth regarded as a fighter unit. Further Blenheim reinforcements for opposing the Italian invasion included 84 Squadron which arrived at

Eulesis on 8 November (A Flight only), and by the end of the month was at full squadron strength based at Menidi (formerly named Tatoi) in Greece. In the same month 211 Squadron flew in to be based at Menidi; while further Blenheim units were to come at the start of 1941.

Meantime in Egypt British forces under the command of General Wavell where being reinforced for an imminent 'reconnaissance in strength' against the Italian armies in North Africa, commencing on 9 December. Air support for this offensive included Nos 11 and 39 Squadrons, sent from Aden for this operation, and Nos 45, 55 and 113 Squadrons — all Blenheim units. By mid-January 1941 Wavell's brilliant advance had proved highly successful in forcing his Italian opponent's forces to retreat westwards rapidly, and No 11 Squadron — by then beginning to receive Mk IVs — was 'released' and took its Blenheims to Greece where it became based at Larissa. No 45 Squadron was also earmarked for Greece but in the event remained in North Africa, while 39 Squadron began replacing its Blenheims with Martin Marylands from January 1941. In March 1941 No 113 Squadron began to move to Greece, and was initially based with 84 Squadron at Menidi. No 113's operational role thereafter wsa photo-reconnaissance sorties along the northern border with Yugoslavia and Bulgaria in anticipation of any imminent moves by German forces towards

Above:
Trio of Mk Is of 55 Squadron (nearest L8397 and L8398) at Ismailia, Egypt mid-1940. *S. W. Lee*

Below:
Blenheim Is of 84 Squadron, 1940. Second from right, L1378 was lost in action on 15 November 1940. *IWM*

Above:
Mk IV, N3589 of 40 Squadron which landed in error on Pantelleria island on 13 September 1940, repainted in Italian markings. *Dr G. F. Ghergo*

Below:
Blenheim V, BA490, 'A-2' of 8 Squadron after a forced landing. *via RAF Museum*

Greece. By April the full squadron complement was in Greece and No 113's crews reverted to normal bombing sorties, moving north to Niamata, a few miles east of Larissa. On 6 April the long-expected move by German forces into Greece commenced, supported by strong Luftwaffe elements greatly outnumbering the RAF strength in Greece. Though retaliatory raids against this invasion were immediately flown by the RAF, the ensuing few weeks became a saga of immense courage as the aircrews fought against hopeless odds in the air.

One survivor from the intense air campaign of April 1941 was Stanley Lee, a Wop/AG serving with 113 Squadron, who has recorded:

'The Germans invaded and we were kept pretty busy although the weather was grim and as big a danger as the Jerries. On 15 April the weather brightened and we were well and truly dealt with by the Luftwaffe. We had five large raids that day on our grass airfield. Bombing and strafing by Ju88s, Me109s and Me110s (sic). By mid-day we'd lost every one of our aircraft, most of our transport, fuel supplies and stores — the lot. Our tents were riddled and we spent the rest of the day crouching in ditches. At dusk we started our mini-Dunkirk, first back to Athens, then Corinth, Argos and then, courtesy of the Royal Navy, to Crete (Suda Bay and then Maleme airfield). Together with other aircrew I left Crete in a 230 Squadron Sunderland to Alexandria.

The following day saw the start of the airborne landings in Crete and most of our groundcrews never made it back. The groundcrews had already suffered casualties in Greece, especially during those last few days at Argos. The campaign in Greece had cost us a lot, if not most, of our ground staff, all our aircraft and equipment, but not one aircrew member.'

In mid-May 113 Squadron reformed at Ramleh, Palestine by acquiring a mixture of fighter and bomber Blenheims from 55 Squadron, then returned to Ma'aten Bagush, Egypt to continue operations in Libya.

The other Greek-based Blenheim squadrons suffered equally traumatic experiences during their bitter, last-ditch operations. On 13 April, for example, six Blenheims of 211 Squadron set out on a bombing sortie — none returned. Jumped by a mass of Messerschmitt Bf109s, every Blenheim was shot down, with only two crew members managing to take to their parachutes. The two survivors managed to return to Larissa by foot, mule and lorry — a journey of some 150 miles — and were offered seats in two Lysanders about to fly south. On take-off the Lysanders were strafed by Bf109s and both shot down, killing one of the 211 Squadron survivors, and shooting two fingers off the hand of the other. Days later the sole member was admitted to an Athens hospital — it was 211 Squadron's last sortie in Greece. On 18 April the Blenheim fighters of 30 Squadron withdrew from Greece to Crete, in order to continue protection patrols over the gathering Allied ships intending to evacuate Allied forces from Greece. In Crete by the end of April the few remaining Blenheims of Nos 11, 84 and 211 Squadrons began being ferried back to Egypt,

though five Blenheim IVFs from 203 Squadron had
by then arrived from Aden to help in protection of
the evacuation. Early in May these and the surviving
Blenheims of 30 Squadron were also withdrawn from
Crete.

While the tragedy of Greece dominated much of
the Blenheim squadrons' activities during the spring
of 1941, it was by no means the only facet of their
operations within the Middle East Command:
12 May saw the real beginning of German assaults
on the battered Allied 'garrison' on Crete, and
Blenheim crews based in Egypt flew bombing sorties
against German positions on the island. Among
these were Blenheim IVs of No 14 Squadron, which
had arrived at Heliopolis, Egypt from the Sudan in
April 1941, having already participated in the anti-
Italian campaign waged in East Africa. Having flown
its first North African sorties against Axis forces
along the Egyptian border — and lost five of a formation to German Bf109s in a single sortie — 14
Squadron next joined in an assault on Luftwaffe
Junkers Ju52 transports on Maleme airfield, destroying at least a dozen Ju52s on 25 May, but losing
three more Blenheims during a similar attack later.
Next day the squadron suffered two more Blenheims
lost, along with two from 55 Squadron, over the
besieged island.

While the disastrous campaigns in Greece and
Crete were at a high peak, and Wavell's initial
successful offensive in North Africa was rapidly
reversed by reinforcement of the Italian armies by

German forces a further threat to the tenuous Allied
grip of the Middle East theatre erupted in Iraq. Pro-
-Axis elements of the Iraqi hierarchy, including four
army generals, banded under the leadership of one
Raschid Ali, forced a coup d'etat in early April 1941,
causing the lawful regent to be flown to safety by the
RAF to the RAF station at Habbaniyah, home of
No 4 Flying Training School (FTS), some 50 miles
west of Baghdad. Since Raschid Ali and his cohorts
were known to be in German pay, this change of
regime posed an immediate threat to access by the
Allies to the oil sources of Persia and Iraq and
virtually opened the roads to India, Egypt and
southern Russia to Germany. Allied reaction was
relatively swift, and on 18 April a contingent of
British and Indian troops disembarked at Basra,
supported by some 400 British troops flown in to
Shaibah from Karachi by No 31 Squadron RAF.
Further Allied troops being convoyed by sea were
due at Basra by 28 April, despite Raschid Ali's
expressed refusal for permission to do so. Accordingly, Iraqi troops in strength moved to surround
RAF Habbaniyah, occupying a nearby plateau offer-
ing a commanding position for their artillery in the
night hours of 30 April.

Well outnumbered in ground forces, the FTS had

Above:
L6670, an ex-203 Squadron machine (seen here as UQ-R of 211 Squadron in the Greek campaign) which went to the Royal Hellenic Air Force on 1 April 1941.

Below:
An 84 Squadron Mk 1 crash-landed at Menidi, Greece in March 1941. *S. W. Lee*

Above:
**Sgt (later, Flt Lt AFC, DFM) S. W. Lee in Blenheim
T2177 of 113 Squadron, 1940.** *S. W. Lee*

only a wide variety of aircraft with which to counter
any assault by the Iraqis. These aircraft, amounting
to little more than 60, were mainly Audax biplanes,
Airspeed Oxfords and a few Gloster Gladiators —
all training machines. All were hastily converted to
carry bombs and machine guns, though their crews
comprised a handful of staff instructors and mostly
aircrew trainees. Requests for reinforcements from
Egypt were made, though the retreats from Libya
and Crete were already pressing hard upon the
RAF's aircraft strength there. In the meantime, at
first light on 2 May, No 4 FTS took off en masse to
attack the Iraqi guns ranged no more than 1,000
yards from the aerodrome, while transport aircraft

began evacuating women and children. Ten Wellingtons of 70 Squadron had by then arrived at Shaibah
from Egypt, and were soon engaged in bombing the
Iraqi artillery positions, while more Wellingtons of
37 Squadron also flew in to Shaibah and were soon
refuelled, bombed up and despatched to the Habbaniyah siege. By the end of the day FTS crews had
flown 193 sorties, constantly taking off under
shellfire and lost five aircraft destroyed and 20 others
rendered unserviceable.

On 3 May Blenheim IVs of 203 Squadron arrived
at Habbaniyah and were quickly involved in the day
and night assaults on the Iraqi guns. On the same
day six Blenheim IVs from Nos 84 and 203
Squadrons joined other forces being gathered
together at H4, a pumping station on the Trans-
Jordan branch of the main oil pipeline. The purpose
of the H4 force was primarily to prevent the landing

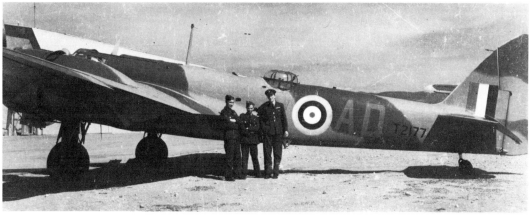

Top:
113 Squadron Blenheim and crew prior to a sortie from Ma'aten Bagush, Egypt. *IWM*

Above:
Blenheim IV, T2177 of 113 Squadron at Menidi (Tatoi), Athens in March 1941. L-R: Sgts J. T. Latimer and S. W. Lee, Plt Off A. S. Grumbley. *S. W. Lee*

grounds at Rutbah and H3, across the border, being utilised by Luftwaffe aircraft known to be en route to assist the Iraqi revolutionary army. The siege of 4 FTS continued until the night of 5/6 May when, in the night hours, the Iraqi artillery and other forces occupying the plateau overlooking Habbaniyah withdrew. Though it meant immediate relief from constant shelling for the FTS inhabitants, it also provided an opportunity for the FTS aircraft and crews to extend their air offensive in constant pursuit of the

retreating Iraqis — an offensive spearheading an Allied troop advance which ultimately caused Raschid Ali to flee the country and allowed official reinstatement of the Regent on 1 June.

To the northwest of Iraq yet another threat existed during those fateful early months of 1941. Syria, a French-administered colony now under the aegis of the French Vichy government, might easily have become another springboard for Axis occupation of the Iraqi and Persian oilfields, as well as a pathway to further conquests east and southwards. While the Allied forces on Crete were still engaged in attempting to thwart the German airborne invasion of that island, and Raschid Ali's army was trying to oust the Allies from Iraq, Admiral Darlan, Foreign Minister in the French Vichy government, calmly agreed to permit Axis aircraft 'refuelling facilities' on Syrian airfields, to provide the Axis with military intelligence

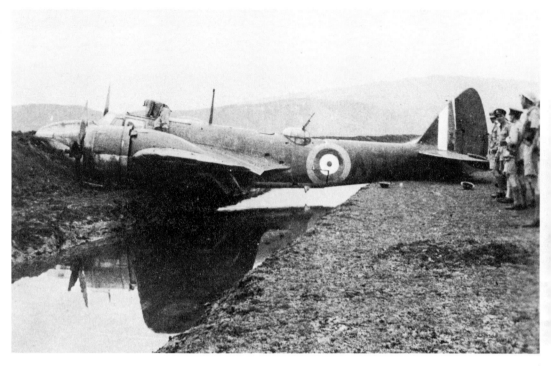

Above:
Return from a sortie. 113 Squadron Mk IV at Niamata, Greece, April 1941. *S. W. Lee*

Below:
T2177 of 113 Squadron in Greece, spring 1941. *S. W. Lee*

Above:
**Blenheim IV, AD-J of 113 Squadron at El Adem, 1941
after a Luftwaffe strafe of the former Italian airfield.**
via RAF Museum

Below:
**113 Squadron Mk IV fitted with ground-strafing 20mm
Hispano cannon; a local modification adopted by several
Blenheim units in North Africa.** *V. Cashmore*

Above and opposite:
Three successive views of strafing an Italian MT convoy on the coast road south of Benghazi, taken from the nose of Blenheim IV, Z5867 of 113 Squadron (pilot, Vic Cashmore) on 26 October 1941. *V. Cashmore*

on Allied movements and, incidentally, to supply arms and munitions to the Iraqi rebels. Knowledge of these intentions led to the RAF establishing a small force of aircraft at H4 pumping station, as previously mentioned, and early on 14 May Flg Off Anthony Watson of 203 Squadron based at H4 reconnoitred Palmyra airfield and spotted a Junkers Ju90 transport aircraft there, plus a number of other Luftwaffe transports during a later recce the same day. That evening Watson, in Blenheim T1820, took off again, accompanied by two Blenheims from 84 Squadron, with a pair of 250 Squadron Curtiss Tomahawks as fighter escort. These bombed and strafed Palmyra, then repeated the attack mid-morning on the following day. Further Blenheim sorties were flown over the next few days, attacking airfields at Palmyra and Nerobaifil, with some success in the destruction of grounded Luftwaffe and Italian aircraft.

It was during a bombing sortie against Rutbah that Flg Off Tony Watson saw a fellow Blenheim shot down. Despite flak damage to his own aircraft (including a ruptured fuel tank) Watson immediately landed alongside the burning wreckage of his companion, retrieved the downed pilot, searched for the other crew members (in vain) despite flame and exploding ammunition, then took off again — all the time under close fire from a gaggle of enemy armoured cars. For this unselfish action Watson received a DFC award in July 1941. On 24 May the handful of 84 Squadron Blenheims at H4 left to join the 4 FTS and other RAF aircraft pursuing retreating rebel Iraqi forces, but the remaining 203

Squadron was reinforced by No 11 Squadron at Aqir, where unit personnel took possession of eight Blenheims from 84 Squadron and six more from 211 Squadron (though 10 of these Blenheims were unserviceable at the time of transfer to No 11). Nevertheless, 11 Squadron commenced operations over Syria on 28 May with a photo-recce sortie over Syrian airfields. The Vichy French response to these Allied moves was to reinforce existing French air strength in Syria by flying in a unit of Dewoitine D520 fighters to Rayak airfield from Algeria.

By the end of May 1941, with the defeat of the Iraqi revolution and the possibility of imminent Allied air attacks against Syria, the Vichy French High Commissioner, Henri Dentz, considered it necessary to request that all German forces in the country be evacuated and that Germany cease utilising Syrian airfields and facilities — a request acceded to by 8 June.

On the same date the Allied armies commenced an invasion of Syria from Palestine and Trans-Jordan, their opposition being the Vichy French army and air force, both of which were to provide intense fighting throughout the subsequent campaign. The Syrian struggle was to last until an official 'cease-fire' on 12 July, followed by a formal armistice on 14 July,

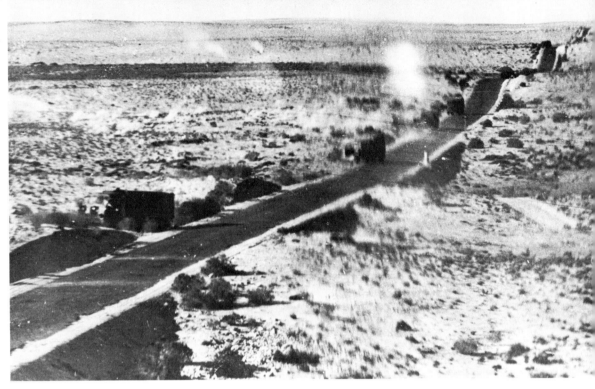

Blenheim OB-A of 45 Squadron over Agordat.
via RAF Museum

Left:
Setting out. 113 Squadron on a sortie over the Western Desert. *S. W. Lee*

Above:
Wg Cdr J. Buchanan DSO, DFC, OC 14 Squadron (centre) January 1942 at Gambut.

Below:
Blenheim IVs of 14 Squadron over typical desert terrain. *via RAF Museum*

when the Vichy French forces capitulated and (in the main) withdrew from the country, leaving it in Allied hands. Blenheims played a not insignificant part in the aerial conflict. The units involved were Nos 11 and 84 Squadrons, joined on 21 June by 45 Squadron, and these units provided the bulk of bombing or photo-recce sorties throughout the campaign. Inevitably a few were lost in action — at least eight being shot down, two others crashlanding after combat, a further two being lost in an air collision and others receiving serious damage. Perhaps the worst single defeat came on 10 July, when 12 Blenheims of 45 Squadron set out to bomb an ammunition dump near Hama, escorted by seven Tomahawks. Having scored many accurate hits on the dump, the Blenheims were then attacked from in front and below by five Dewoitine D520s, which shot down three Blenheims in quick succession, severely damaged a fourth which had to belly-land later and caused serious damage to six other Blenheims. Once the armistice was declared most RAF units returned to Egypt, but 84 Squadron remained based at Mosul, Iraq as part of the garrison force, moving base to Habbaniyah in September 1941, then joining its companion Blenheim units in Egypt in October when it moved to Amiriya. No 11 Squadron moved from Habbaniyah to Landing Ground 09, Egypt in September 1941, while 45 Squadron became based on LG16, Egypt (Fuka's satellite) in the same month. No 203 Squadron, which had provided valuable preliminary aid to the campaign, had moved from Habbaniyah to Kabrit on the Suez Canal on 29 May,

there to resume its former role of maritime reconnaissance between Crete and Libya.

With the eastern end of the Mediterranean theatre virtually secure, the Allied air commanders could now concentrate their attention wholly on Libya, Malta and the general North African battle scenes. Vital to any future plans for any Allied offensive along the Libyan coast was the question of preventing Rommel's Afrika Korps and its Italian allies receiving supplies via shipping convoys in the Mediterranean, and the key to this problem was the strategically located island of Malta. Among the various Malta-based units during 1941 were detachments of UK-based Blenheim squadrons. These, from No 2 Group, had commenced on 26 April when six crews from 21 Squadron started from England to fly to Malta, via Gibraltar, as a 'testing flight'. Once at Malta they flew a few sorties, then returned to England to report on conditions. Having thus 'proved' the possibility for Blenheims to reach and operated from Malta, plans were initiated for certain Blenheim units of No 2 Group to 'rotate' in 5/6-week detachments to the island, there to assist in Malta's aerial anti-shipping offensive in the Mediterranean. First to go was No 82 Squadron in two formations, leaving the UK on 4 and 11 June respectively, flying 'tropicalised' Mk IVs. Once on Malta little time was wasted in getting operational. On 22 June six of 82's Blenheims attacked an enemy convoy off Lampedusa, seriously damaging one vessel but running a gauntlet of flak and fighters. Piloting Blenheim Z9545, 'B', Flt Lt T. J. Watkins

Above left:
Desert Air Force Blenheims with Kittyhawk escort (nearest bomber, Z5893). *IWM*

Above:
Z5860 closing up. *IWM*

Below:
Sand-boys. Cheerful Blenheim crews aboard *Joy*, evidently an aircraft with an Australian skipper.

This page, opposite and overleaf:
Varying views of the Free French 'Lorraine' Squadron in North Africa. Note differing styles of painting the *Croix de Lorraine* unit marking and full-length rudder tri-colour banding.
Cinema video des Armees, Paris & via R. C. B. Ashworth

Blenheim IV of 39 Squadron about to be moved by road from Alexandria to Aboukir, Egypt because of bogged airfield, 1941.
W. J. Laxton via P. H. T. Green

suffered a near-severed leg from one flak burst, and his navigator Sgt Sargent managed the controls until arriving back over Luqa, when Watkins, in great agony, accomplished a safe landing then collapsed. Watkins and Sargent received immediate awards of a DSO and DFM respectively. Sargent was, some three months later, to repeat his actions by again taking over control of a Blenheim with a wounded pilot, this time landing the aircraft.

Having suffered a high casualty rate, 82 Squadron's survivors made their way back to England in July, to be replaced by 110 Squadron, which flew out starting on 1 July. Eight days later 110 Squadron flew its first sorties, hitting three 7-12,000ton ships in Tripoli harbour. On 13 July its crews destroyed three more vessels, and next day attacked a Luftwaffe airstrip in Libya, destroying a Ju52 in the process. The unit's next victim was an 8,000-tonner on 15 July, but on 20 July, while bombing the power station at Tripoli, it met fierce opposition. On return from this sortie the unit commander, Wg Cdr T. M. Hunt, was fired on from long range by an Italian fighter and was shot down into the sea. Further successes came on 22 July (two ships destroyed), while next day four Blenheims

destroyed two more in Trapani harbour, then rounded out the trip by strafing a nearby airfield. The sortie leader, Sgt Cathles, twice hit the sea on the outward flight but completed his attack before force-landing in enemy territory. On 28 July the squadron returned to the UK, being 'exchanged' with No 105 Squadron, led by Wg Cdr Hughie Edwards VC, DFC, which reached Luqa on that date.

On 31 July, led by Edwards, 105 Squadron made its initial operation, when six crews attempted to attack an escorted convoy northeast of Pantelleria, but was driven off by Italian fighters. They were more successful on 7 August, sinking four of six ships; while on the 15th five Blenheim crews of 105 Squadron destroyed two escorted tankers between Tripoli and Benghazi. Tragically, one Blenheim received a direct flak hit and disintegrated in midair, a second hit a ship's mast and dived into the sea, while a third fell victim to machine gun fire. By this time enemy ships were being fitted with plentiful gun defences and casualty rates among the attacking RAF aircraft were averaging some 12%, or virtually the loss of one crew per day on overall average. On-the-spot replacements came from other Blenheim crews ostensibly ferrying aircraft to Egypt via Malta. Other reinforcement came at the end of August when 26 crews of No 107 Squadron left Portreath bound for Malta, and began Mediterranean operations on 15 September. Such was the desperate priority for maintaining the anti-shipping offensive against Rommel's supply routes that Nos 105 and 107 Squadrons

Above:
Trainer. L8391, '14' of the Ismailia OTU, Egypt which had previously flown with 55 and 211 Squadrons, and by January 1942 was at Nanyuki, Kenya. *V. Cashmore*

Below:
203 Squadron's Blenheims over a Syrian landscape, 1941. *IWM*

Above:
Blenheim V, EH495 in North Africa early 1943. *H. Levy*

Below:
R3844, a veteran Blenheim which saw service with 59, 105, 88, 21, 14 and 162 Squadrons before finally being 'retired' on 1 February 1944. Seen here at Kabrit, Egypt. *H. Levy*

Above:
Blenheim V, BA336 in Egypt, 1943.

remained on Malta long after their nominal '5/6-week tour'.

Each sortie now became an increasing hazard as enemy flak and fighter opposition were strengthened, and the casualty rate among the Blenheim crews rose alarmingly. Wg Cdr Harte, 107's commander, was lost on 9 October, while his temporary successor, Sqn Ldr Barnes, was posted 'Missing' only days later; indeed, by November every commissioned officer on 107 Squadron was either dead, missing or repatriated, and the command of the unit was in the hands of Sgt Ivor Broom, who was commissioned as Plt Off on the spot. (He was later to rise to Air Rank and awarded the DSO, DFC and AFC.) On 105 Squadron Hughie Edwards returned to the UK and was succeeded as commander by Wg Cdr D. W. Scivier on 31 August, but on 22 September, during a low-level strafe of the Tripoli-Benghazi coastal road, Scivier's Blenheim lost its tail in a collision with another Blenheim. Command of 105 Squadron passed to Wg Cdr P. H. A. Simmons DFC on 1 October. October also saw the arrival of part of No 18 Squadron, which remained on the island until transferring to Egypt in January 1942.

Throughout October 1941 — when Malta became the daily target for a sustained Luftwaffe onslaught — to February 1942, the Blenheim crews battled on, dividing their attentions between anti-shipping sorties and straight bombing/strafing onslaughts on enemy airfields, installations and troops. One example of the latter land objectives was the Sicilian airfield at Castel Vetrano, which was attacked by 10 Blenheims from 18 and 107 Squadrons (the total serviceable aircraft available from these units) on 4 January 1942. Arriving over their target in the late afternoon, the Blenheims achieved almost total surprise and duly bombed and gunned the field, destroyed at least 30 enemy aircraft on the ground and damaging others. This raid almost coincided with the return to

Malta of 21 Squadron, which arrived at the height of the German assault. Despite ultra-primitive messing and accommodation conditions, and the daily bombing of Malta's airfields and dispersals, the Blenheim crews continued to operate. On 4 February an anti-shipping sweep went astray due to navigational error and three of the six No 21 Squadron aircraft crashed into mountains; while on 11 February another formation returning from the Gulf of Gabes was intercepted by German fighters over Malta, losing one Blenheim into the sea. By the end of the month the Blenheims' 'Malta Saga' was over. No 21 Squadron was disbanded on 14 March (though officially reformed at Bodney, England on the same date); 107 Squadron too was 'reformed' in England; 18 Squadron personnel and aircraft were absorbed into other Middle East units, and a 'new' squadron formed at Wattisham with fresh crews; while 105 Squadron personnel had already arrived back in England (Swanton Morley, Norfolk) on 11 October there to be soon re-equipped with de Havilland Mosquito bombers.

The gathering of Blenheim units in Egypt towards the end of 1941 was one facet of a general 'beefing-up' of Allied air strength in preparation for Operation 'Crusader' — the intended strongest Allied offensive to date in North Africa, and due to commence in November. On 15 November 1941 — just three days before 'Crusader' was launched — the preliminary air offensive, primarily aimed at enemy airstrips to nullify Luftwaffe interference, got under way. On that date the following units were flying Blenheims: Nos 8 (a detachment only), 11, 14, 45, 55, 84, 113 and the Free French 'Lorraine' Squadrons. While most were 'straight' Mk IVs, No 113 Squadron had 'converted' many of its aircraft to 'ground-strafers' by installing a long-barrel 20mm Hispano cannon forward, protruding through the lower starboard window of the nose section. As such the Squadron's primary function was low-level scouring of the long coastal road of enemy vehicles and troop movements, with 'side-show' attacks on any airfields or landing strips adjacent. The subsequent success of this form of Blenheim offensive armament was to be adopted by other units later. Once 'Crusader' was under way, the struggle for air supremacy over the battle zones became fiercely contested between the Luftwaffe and the Western Desert Air Force (WDAF), reaching a particular peak on 22 November when the slender German fighter force made its most determined attempt to break the numerically-superior Allied air force. That morning Blenheims of 45 Squadron, escorted by Tomahawks of No 3 Squadron RAAF, clashed with a formation of Messerschmitt Bf109s, and quickly lost four Blenheims and three Tomahawks. By the end of the day, despite heavy losses on both sides, the WDAF had clearly demonstrated its ability to hold its own in any close engagements; virtually the starting-point of Allied air supremacy over the North African desert.

During the ensuing weeks, as the land battle raged below, the Blenheim squadrons were out daily, heavily escorted, bombing and strafing forward enemy troops and airfields and incurring many casualties. Then, in early December, came news of Japan's undeclared entry into the war on the side of the Axis powers when its forces struck simultaneously at Pearl Harbour and Malaya. The overall effect of this development upon the desert air strength was an immediate diversion of reinforcement aircraft, crews, even complete squadrons to the Far East. Of the Blenheim units in the Middle East, Nos 84, 113 and 211 Squadrons left in January 1942, followed in February by No 45 Squadron. Of these, 84 Squadron's air echelon arrived in Sumatra on 23 January; 211 Squadron's 18 aircraft arrived in Sumatra variously between 23 January and 14 February; 113 Squadron went to Toungoo, Burma and 45 Squadron also went initially to Burma. The remaining Blenheim squadrons were soon to relinquish the type. On 16 April 1942 the Free French 'Lorraine' Squadron* ceased operations in North Africa and moved to Syria; while Nos 55 and 14 Squadrons began re-equipment with Baltimores and Marauders in May and August 1942 respectively. This left only 11 Squadron to soldier on with Blenheims, as indeed it was fated to do until being declared non-operational as late as August 1943.

If, by the summer of 1942, the doughty Blenheim was slowly disappearing from firstline use in North Africa, its stablemate development, the Mk V (termed Bisley in contemporary records) was about to enter the same arena. On 7 August No 15 Squadron of the South African Air Force (SAAF) began operations with Mk Vs in the role of coastal anti-shipping and anti-submarine strike, being based at Mariut, with a detachment at Kufra Oasis. Within weeks its crews had several successes, particularly in

attacking German and Italian F-boats. By October 1942, just prior to the battle of El Alamein, the Middle East order of battle showed few units still flying Blenheims, these being 15 Squadron SAAF and 13 (Hellenic) Squadron; the latter having been formed mainly from Greek expatriates for general recce and anti-submarine patrolling duties. Elsewhere around the Mediterranean a handful of Blenheims partially equipped Nos 47, 203 and 244 Squadrons, plus No 1438 Flight. Nevertheless, further units were at that time forming in England; Nos 13, 18, 114 and 614 Squadrons, forming No 326 Wing, were earmarked to fly to Algeria to participate in Operation 'Torch', the Anglo-American invasion of North Africa. All four squadrons were equipped with Blenheim Vs and tasked with a low level army support role, and all arrived at Blida airfield by 18 November and were quickly in action. During the next three months the Mk Vs were in constant action, despite appalling casualties on occasion (see chapter 10) and the obvious defencelessness of the design in the context of any aerial opposition. Such success as was achieved by the Mk Vs can only be attributed to the astounding determination and courage of their crews, rather than the aircraft design. Fortunately, perhaps, the Mk V's sojourn on frontline bombing duties was relatively brief; by the spring of 1943 most had either been exchanged for Bostons, or the squadrons had switched to a relatively safer role of coastal patrol. Apart from an attempt to raise yet another Mk V unit, No 16 Squadron SAAF, in early 1943 — which soon changed to Beauforts — no further Mk V squadrons were formed in the Middle East.

By July 1943 the order of battle prior to the Allied invasion of Sicily showed just five units still operating Blenheims: Nos 13 and 614 Squadrons with the NW African Coastal Force, Nos 13 (Hellenic) and 15 Squadron SAAF on recce and anti-submarine duties, and No 162 Squadron which had a few Blenheim Vs for 'special duties', ie calibration of enemy and Allied radio and radar. The anti-submarine role was continued for a few months by 13 Squadron RAF, including a probable sinking of one U-boat by Flg Off Finch on 12 September, but in October the unit was withdrawn for re-equipment with Venturas, while in the same month No 13 (Hellenic) Squadron exchanged its Mk Vs for Baltimores. No 614 Squadron continued flying its Mk Vs until December 1943, averaging some 80-90 sorties per month, but then ceased operations and was disbanded in February 1944. No 15 Squadron SAAF received its first four Baltimore replacements in June 1943 and by early July had completed the change in aircraft. In effect it was the swan-song of the Blenheim in the Mediterranean theatre of operations, though individual aircraft lingered on as trainers, communication hacks or instructional airframes.

*This unit remained simply titled 'Lorraine' until eventually being called No 342 Squadron with effect from 7 April 1943, by which date it was based in England flying Douglas Bostons.

9
Jungle Warriors

Air power for Britain's prewar Empire territories 'east of Suez' was, at best, little more than a reluctant gesture as far as adequate funding and, particularly, modernisation were concerned by the various governments of the 1920-36 era. Almost traditionally, those RAF squadrons tasked with 'air control' in India and Malaya had to carry out their myriad operational roles with aircraft long out-

moded in design or ability compared with the equipment of UK-based units; an ironic situation when it is realised that the overseas squadrons of that era seldom enjoyed any lengthy period of service *without* being embroiled in 'sharp end' operational flying. In India, in 1938, for example, were just eight firstline squadrons Nos 5, 11, 20, 27, 28, 31, 39 and 60 — all equipped with biplanes of varying vintage. Occasionally, single examples of more modern aircraft designs appeared on the Indian scene, primarily early production or prototype machines attached to squadrons to undergo tropical trials, but actual re-equipment with up-dated monoplane aircraft was slow.

A year later, just prior to the outbreak of war in Europe, this state of RAF affairs had improved inasmuch as three squadrons — Nos 11, 39 and 60

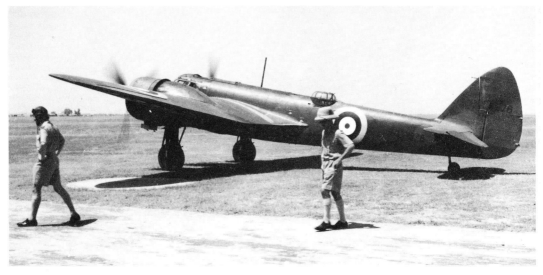

Above:
L8376, which later served with 60 Squadron at Risalpur, India on 2 August 1939. *Sqn Ldr L. W. Davies FRGS*

Below:
L4911, AD-H of 60 Squadron at Ambala, 3 October 1939. It also served with 11 and 27 Squadrons.
Sqn Ldr L. W. Davies FRGS

— had already begun conversion to Blenheim I bombers; while in August 1939 No 62 Squadron flew from its base at Cranfield, Bedfordshire to Singapore and by the end of September was fully established at Tengah airfield on that island, where it was joined by another ex-UK Blenheim I unit, No 34 Squadron from Watton, Norfolk, in the same month. Of the other resident India units, No 27 Squadron began its second World War still equipped with ageing Westland Wapiti biplanes and did not begin to receive Blenheims until January 1941; while No 20 Squadron had to wait until June 1941 before receiving a handful of Blenheim Is to supplement the Westland Lysanders already received in the previous February, although in the following December these Blenheims were relinquished and the squadron became an all-Lysander unit. Meanwhile, No 11 Squadron had left the Far East theatre in June 1940, going first to Aden, then in December 1940 moving northwest to Egypt. Thus, by 8 December 1941 — when Japanese assault troops first set foot ashore in Malaya — there remained merely four Blenheim squadrons in the Malayan Peninsula and Singapore: Nos 27, 34, 60 and 62, based respectively at Sungei Patani, Tengah, Kuantan and Alor Star. All were flying Blenheim I bombers* except 27 Squadron which had, since February 1941, been designated as a 'night-fighter' unit — then the sole unit performing such a role in the Far East — and accordingly had converted its Mk Is to Mk IFs by adding a four-gun belly pack, and, incidentally, giving each aircraft an overall black livery in the spring of 1941. Each of the four units held an operational establishment of 12 aircraft as a norm, and this operational total of at least 48 Blenheims was 'supported' by a further 17 machines held in 'reserve' awaiting future issue when needed.

As indicated by their locations, Nos 27, 34 and 62 Squadrons, along with No 21 Squadron RAAF (Brewster Buffalos) at Sungei Patani, comprised

*Though 34 Squadron had received a few Mk IVs early in 1941.

'Norgroup', the air defence formation of northern Malaya, and were therefore literally in the 'frontline' of any incursion by the Japanese via neutral Siam or the eastern Malayan coastline, while No 60 Squadron was based further southeast along the Pahang coast as a 'halfway stop' frontline unit. In the early hours of 8 December (local dateline) Japan struck simultaneously at Singapore city and began landing invasion forces at Kota Bahru, with their main force going ashore at Singora, Siam. The Kota Bahru landing was in effect a feint thrust aimed at attracting the Allied defence aircraft away from the prime invasion point of Singora, and in this it succeeded immediately. No 27 Squadron received orders to bomb and strafe shipping in the Kota Bahru area 'at first light', and all 12 Blenheims took off at dawn only to run into blinding rainstorms which precluded any sighting of a target. Returning to Sungei Patani their Blenheims were in the process of refuelling when, at 7am, the Operations Room warned of approaching unidentified aircraft from the east. Within minutes a formation of Japanese aircraft hove in sight and began bombing. No 27's crews, still with their aircraft, never received the warning and their first indication was a salvo of fragmentation and incendiary bombs crashing among the static Blenheims. Within a mere seven minutes eight of the 12 Blenheims had been rendered useless, the airfield riddled with craters, buildings set afire, and numerous casualties lay among the desolation. A second raid at 10.45am repeated the process of destruction, though the four remaining Blenheims of 27 Squadron escaped any further serious damage. Despite trojan efforts by the surviving personnel to make the airfield usable again, orders were received for the RAF units to withdraw to Butterworth, which was accomplished next day.

At Butterworth the incoming personnel found

Below:
New arrivals at Madras being inspected keenly.
Sqn Ldr L. W. Davies FRGS

similar conditions because it too had been bombed thoroughly on 8 December. As 27 Squadron's survivors worked without halt to service and prepare their remaining Blenheims, a Japanese force of 27 bombers appeared over Butterworth at 5pm and completed the destruction of the airfield. At the other end of the airstrip No 34 Squadron, which had lost three from a six-aircraft formation attacking the Japanese-occupied Singora airfield earlier that morning, suffered further casualties, while a surprise attack on the grounded Blenheims of 62 Squadron at Alor Star decimated them, leaving the sole airborne Blenheim, piloted by Sqn Ldr A. S. K. Scarf, to set out on a desperately courageous lone sortie to Singora (see chapter 10). In the evening of 9 December, the 'Norgroup' commander, Wg Cdr R. G. Forbes, ordered a complete withdrawal of his air units from the northern airfields with the ultimate objective of regrouping all surviving aircraft and crews on Singapore island.

The other Blenheim unit, No 60 Squadron at Kuantan Airfield — which it shared with No 8 Squadron RAAF (Lockheed Hudsons) — was actually a detachment of eight Blenheims and crews flown in at the end of November, the main squadron base then being at Mingaladon, Burma. Plt Off (later, Wg Cdr) P. N. Kingwill, an observer/navigator with 60 Squadron's Kuantan detachment at that time, described the events of 8/9 December:*

'On the night of the 7th the Station Commander came into the Mess, told me to get all the aircraft armed and be ready to take off at 07.00hrs next morning to attack shipping off the coast of Kota Bahru. We were also told we need not expect any air opposition. That was the sum total of our briefing. We were ready and loaded with four 250lb bombs to take off at dawn. I think we got seven of the eight off. We flew in loose formation, Dick Vivian† in the lead.

*Sixty Squadron'; D. W. Warne/A. J. Young; 1967.

† Wg Cdr R. L. Vivian, OC Squadron.

Above left:
Blenheim Is of the Ambala Conversion Flight on the annual AOC's Inspection Parade, 18 March 1940.
Sqn Ldr L. W. Davies FRGS

Left:
New arrivals (nearest, L1545) alongside 27 Squadron's Wapiti IIAs, Madras, 1939. L1545 went to 60 Squadron and was lost over the Bay of Bengal on 30 August 1940. *MoD (Air)*

Above:
L4827 of 60 Squadron over the Punjab, 11 July 1940. It crashed at Victoria Point, Burma on 16 September 1941. *Sqn Ldr L. W. Davies FRGS*

We were to carry out independent low level attacks on any enemy ships we could find. Off Kota Bahru there was a 10/15,000ton transport already on fire. There were numerous landing craft moving to and from the beach. Vivian flew around out at sea to size up the situation. Two or three Blenheims decided to drop their bombs on the transport. We followed in behind and could see that she was red-hot inside, with bodies sprawled all over the decks. We decided not to waste our bombs on it . . . Vivian picked out a group of landing craft as a target. We dropped our bombs in a stick across them, but by the time the 20-second fuzes had burned the craft had moved some yards away. We could see the crews firing at us with automatic weapons. One of the boats overturned in the explosion which followed and the others must have been badly shaken. It was a neat bit of bombing but not very effective.'

Despite the briefing there was heavy air opposition and, having dropped their bombs, the crews hurriedly returned to Kuantan. Kingwill continued: 'Dobson* arrived much later and it turned out he

*Flg Off J. A. B. Dobson.

was the only one to locate the main Japanese landing force, having flown north up the coast to Thailand (Siam). He had attacked two warships and had met the full force of their defensive armament. Fortunately, he got away without being hit. Two aircraft failed to return from this first raid. Westropp-Bennett† was shot down, crashed on the beach, and he and his crew were all killed. We stood by for the rest of the day, but there was no second defensive sortie.'

On 9 December No 60 Squadron's detachment was ordered to pull out and proceed to Tengah, Singapore. Only four Blenheims were left to make the flight.

The experiences of the 27 and 60 Squadrons' crews were common to all RAF and RAAF units, and the mass withdrawal south to Singapore was soon under way. Official records surviving indicate, for one example, that No 27 Squadron was 'withdrawn and regrouped at Kallang airport, Singapore on 12 December'; in fact, merely a scratch collection of Blenheim Is from various sources became 'based' at Kallang and operated spasmodically at night as 'fighters', though with little effect. The last four Blenheims, their crews and two spare pilots of 60 Squadron's Kuantan detachment arrived at Tengah in the morning of 9 December, in the wake of a heavy air raid which had left Tengah's sole runway cratered. Though without sleep for days, the crews were ordered to man three Mk IVs of 34 Squadron and, with three more 34 Squadron Blenheims, to bomb targets in the Singora area. As there was insufficient fuel for a return flight to Singapore, they

†Sqn Ldr G. P. Westropp-Bennett. The other casualty was Plt Off W. W. Bowden whose Blenheim was shot into the sea, killing his crew, though Bowden was retrieved by a Japanese destroyer and became a prisoner for the rest of the war.

were to land 'where they could'. All six crews took off, reached Singora and attacked a mass of Japanese shipping despite a murderous gun barrage, and were then chased back over the Malayan border by a host of enemy fighters. Five Blenheims went down into the jungle, and only one, piloted by Flt Lt J. W. Appleton, survived to land at Butterworth and later return to Tengah. There, with only six Blenheims between 60 and 34 Squadrons, the remaining crews flew more sorties against the advancing Japanese forces. On the night of 12 December, Appleton of 60 Squadron crashed on take-off, was taken to hospital, and was later captured and imprisoned by the Japanese. On 23 December the 60 Squadron survivors handed their remaining aircraft, plus some aircrew members, to the remnants of 34 and 62 squadron, and these latter flew to Sumatra to continue the struggle. Next day the 60 Squadron crews left in Singapore, without any aircraft, embarked on the ss *Darvel* and sailed for Rangoon.

The final bitter defence was relatively brief. On 8 February 1942 Japanese troops invaded Singapore island from Johore, two days later the last RAF fighters were evacuated to Sumatra, and on 15 February Singapore surrendered. Only three days later Sumatra became untenable and remaining Allied forces there withdrew to Java and continued their fight until 8 March, on which date the Dutch authorities surrendered to the invading Japanese. Such are the succinct facts, but these give little hint

of the heroic efforts made against daunting odds by the constantly dwindling RAF and RAAF units in Sumatra and Java. Australian official records state, 'Between 23rd and 27th of January (1942) three RAF squadrons, Nos 27 (Night-fighter), 34 and 62 (Bomber), has also been transferred to Sumatra', yet the description of those remnant units as 'squadrons' was simply a literary kindness. Between all three they could not muster the normal fighting strength of one squadron, while 27 Squadron's 'contribution' was known to be only three well-patched Blenheims. The RAAF account also fails to include the Blenheims and air crews of No 84 Squadron which arrived from Egypt in Sumatra on 23 January, moving to P2 airfield next day. P2 and P1 airstrips were situated south and north respectively of Palembang, from which the besieged RAF units fought on until the bitter end, despite constant aerial attacks, lack of maintenance facilities, accommodation and practically every other normal amenity. Merely one example of the toll of RAF aircraft was a Japanese raid against P1 airfield on 7 February, when six Blenheims and three Hurricanes were totally burned, 13 more aircraft seriously damaged, three Hurricanes shot down in the air, and a seventh Blenheim destroyed as it came in to land, its pilot being killed.

P1 airfield succumbed to a Japanese paratroop 'invasion' on 14 February, leaving only P2 airstrip for the bombers to operate from, while on that day a Japanese seaborne invasion force was sighted approaching Sumatra. All available bombers attempted to nullify this latest threat, constantly bombing any incoming convoys for some 48 hours and achieving a modicum of success in destroying

Below:
Blenheim V in India, 1942. *Mod (Air)*

many of the would-be invaders, though at a high cost. Unable to exploit this success, however, the Allied forces withdrew to Java by 18 February. Next day, operating from Kalidjati, five of the six surviving Blenheims attacked enemy shipping at Palembang, repeating their attacks daily for the following week, three Blenheims even claiming a Japanese submarine as sunk on 23 February. Further seaborne Japanese invasion convoys bore in, to be constantly harassed and bombed by the few RAF and RAAF bombers available, but by dawn on 1 March the airfield at Kalidjati was about to be occupied by forward Japanese elements, and so No 84 Squadron's last aircraft were destroyed or captured. The end came suddenly on 8 March when, without consulting the Allied military authorities, General ter Poorten, the Dutch Commander-in-Chief, calmly announced total surrender and ordered all troops to cease fighting. Many RAF men refused privately to accept this capitulation and by myriad methods and routes accomplished remarkable escapes from Japanese imprisonment; none more astonishing than that of Wg Cdr J. R. Jeudwine, OC 84 Squadron who, with three other RAF officers and seven RAAF SNCOs, 'commandeered' a ship's lifeboat in the port of Tjilitjap, named it *Scorpion* (the squadron's official badge motif), then spent 47 days at sea before finally being sighted off Australia and retrieved.

If the struggle for Malaya, Sumatra and Java was over, the battle for India and Burma was only in its infancy. Even as the first Japanese incursions in Siam and Malaya were gaining ground, other Japanese forces were setting out to capture India and Burma. The subsequent massive struggle from December 1941 until the Japanese surrender in

August 1945 has no place in this volume, but the small, though by no means insignificant, part played in that conflict by Blenheims requires description within the context of the Blenheim story. In all, six Blenheim squadrons were directly involved in the India/Burma campaigns — Nos 11, 34, 42, 45, 62 and 113 — each in its individual manner adding lustre to the aircraft's doughty fighting reputation. Of these, No 60 Squadron was already based at Mingaladon, with detachments at Kuantan and Mergui, when Japan invaded Malaya in December 1941, and over the following three months or so was to remain incohesive as a complete unit. In January 1942 60 Squadron's commander, Wg Cdr Vivian, took two officers and 30 men from the unit to Toungoo where, on 7 January, No 113 Squadron commanded by Wg Cdr R. N. Stidolph arrived from the Middle East with 16 Blenheim IVs and absorbed the 60 Squadron personnel from Mingaladon, as well as having all ground maintenance provided by 60 Squadron's 'Erks'. Within hours of arrival at Toungoo, 113 Squadron's crews took off to bomb the Japanese base at Bangkok, dropping some 11,000lb of bombs thereon; while in the following weeks low level bombing and strafing by 113's crews destroyed nearly 60 Japanese aircraft on the ground. Such efforts, however, failed to stem the advancing Japanese, and all Allied forces were forced into a steady retreat to India.

Below:
Blenheim IV, T2251, MU-A of 60 Squadron at Ansonsol in 1942. It had previously seen service with 55 and 113 Squadrons in the Middle East, and was SOC on 9 December 1942. *via Sqn Ldr D. W. Warne*

By the end of February 1942 most Allied air units in Burma had drawn back to Magwe aerodrome, which was promptly raided by Japanese bombers who destroyed most of the grounded aircraft there. Nevertheless, Magwe provided a force of nine Blenheims and 10 Hurricanes for an attack against Japanese-occupied Mingaladon on 21 March, destroying 16 aircraft on the ground and 11 more in the air — two of the latter being victims of the Blenheims' gunners. The heavy retaliatory raids on Magwe by Japanese bombers left merely six flyable Blenheims which were flown to Akyab. By the close of March the Allied retreat was, to all intents and purposes, complete, with surviving Allied forces mainly regrouping and recuperating within India. No 60 Squadron's remaining personnel were gathered at Lahore in early March 1942 where, on 26 March, five elderly Blenheim IVs were flown in as the beginning of complete unit re-equipment on this type. Then after a few weeks of local training, the squadron flew eastwards to its latest operational base at Asansol in India in early May and was soon back in action. No 113 Squadron, which had also ceased operations by March 1942 and been dispersed, was reformed at Asansol, Bengal in April 1942 with Blenheim IVs; while No 34 Squadron reformed at Allahabad, India with Mk IVs in the same month. No 11 Squadron, based at Helwan in Egypt in February 1942, continued its nomadic existence, this time by moving to Colombo, Ceylon in March, flying Blenheim IVs; in the same month another Egyptian-based Blenheim unit, No 45 Squadron, arrived in the Far East, to be technically 'based' at Calcutta, but with operational echelons stationed variously at Lashio, Akyab and Asansol by late March.

By May 1942 the first Burma 'campaign' — albeit primarily a fighting retreat and desperate defensive conflict — was over, and the Allies quickly gathered strength and equipment for the future. Part of that rearmament was reinforcement of the key island of Ceylon (now titled Sri Lanka), where Trincomalee was the British naval base for the Indian Ocean, and which because of the loss of Burma and Rangoon in March now lay wide open for the Japanese naval and air forces should they attempt a second Pearl Harbor-style strike. On 26 March just such a force left Kendari in the Celebes and entered the Indian Ocean, led by Vice-Adm Chuichi Nagumo, the man who had led the Japanese attack on Pearl Harbour only months before. With the Allied knowledge of Japanese secret codes by then, this fresh menace was immediately known to Allied commanders and hasty reinforcement of the air and naval defences of Ceylon was put in hand quickly. Thus by the end of March Ceylon's air strength comprised some 50 Hurricanes, six Catalina flying boats, some Fleet Air Arm Fulmars and Albacores and No 11 Squadron RAF with 14 Blenheim IVs; the latter commanded by Wg Cdr A. J. G. Smyth DFC and based from

24 March on the Colombo Racecourse airstrip.

In the early dawn of 5 April, Easter Sunday, Nagumo's naval force was positioned some 200 miles south of Ceylon, and an aerial strike force of 125 Japanese aircraft, including 'Zero' fighter escorts left their carriers, led by Cdr Mitsuo Fuchida who had led the air attack on Pearl Harbour. Their target was the Allied naval force in harbour, with secondary objectives of a railway workshop and the oil depots east of Colombo. No 11 Squadron's contributions to the subsequent operations against the Japanese began that morning when Wg Cdr Smyth led 10 Blenheims off to locate the enemy naval formation, but failed to find it. A second reconnaissance by the Blenheims on 7 April also failed to establish the enemy fleet's location. Two days later, led by Sqn Ldr Ault, 11 Blenheims took off to attack the now-known position of the enemy naval force. Two Blenheims aborted early with engine problems, but the other nine — without fighter escort — finally found their targets and quickly attacked, despite having to run a gauntlet of patrolling 'Zeros' and anti-aircraft fire. Only four Blenheims returned to base, one with an airscrew shot off, and all displaying the scars of battle. By 10 April the Japanese were withdrawing and the 'Battle of Ceylon' was over.

While the Allied forces in India sweltered under the summer monsoons, and aerial defences for the Indian border cities and territories were slowly strengthened, preparations were already under way for striking back into Burma. Preliminary probing land-offensives were set in motion in December 1942 by the first Arakan campaign, with the ultimate objective of occupying Akyab island in the Bay of Bengal. The RAF spearheaded the campaign by coastal strikes off Akyab and a spasmodic series of bombing/strafing raids against Japanese-held airfields at Magwe and elsewhere, as well as strikes against occupied villages and enemy transport routes. Japanese air opposition was relatively rare, though occasionally fierce, as on 9 September previous to the land offensive, when five Blenheims of 113 Squadron joined with four from 60 Squadron in attacking a shipping convoy near Akyab. One ship was sunk but Japanese 'Zeros' jumped the bombers and shot down two, while three other Blenheims later incurred damage during forced landings. Once the Arakan offensive began to move against the Japanese the Blenheims were moved nearer to the fighting lines; No 60 Squadron, for example, becoming based at Jessore, some 100 miles further forward. Increasing enemy air opposition resulted in greater concentration on attacking such Japanese air bases as Magwe and Toungoo, but as the Blenheims moved further forward more retaliation came from their aerial opponents. By March 1943 several RAF units were based at Dohazari, and on 23 March nine Japanese fighters strafed the airstrip, burning an 11

Squadron Blenheim and damaging five of 60 Squadron's machines, while next day a repeat raid destroyed another Blenheim. By then the Allied armies were withdrawing from the Arakan and the RAF's prime task was to protect these ground forces, at the same time maintaining an offensive 'pressure' on the enemy with bombing and strafing sorties. One of the last such raids prior to ultimate withdrawal to Indian bases took place on 13 May when a force of 35 RAF bombers, with about the same number of Hurricane escorts, attacked Japanese supply dumps at Kappagaung and returned without loss.

By June 1943, and the onset of the summer moonsoon, the Blenheim was recognised as well overdue for replacement in firstline roles. In that month the Order of Battle for the British Air Forces in India and Ceylon showed just five remaining Blenheim-equipped units:

Squadron	Base	Equipment
11	Feni (Fenny)	Blenheim IV
34	Madras	Bleinheim IV (non-operational)
42	Kumbhirgram	Blenheim V
60	Yellahanka	Blenheim IV (non-operational)
113	Feni (Fenny)	Blenheim V

Yet, while awaiting long overdue replacement the ageing Blenheims continued to operate, in the words of the official history:
'... their indomitable ground crews sometimes working for two days at a stretch to make them serviceable, and round the damp tree-fringed airfield of Fenny the phrase 'It will clear in the air' echoed almost as monotonously as the grunt of pain wrung from men tortured by prickly heat who, in default of jacks and winches, hoisted bombs upon their backs so that yet another sortie might be flown'.*

*'RAF 1939-45, vol III'; H. St G. Saunders; HMSO, 1954.

By 1 August 1943, Nos 11, 34 and 60 Squadrons had ceased Blenheim operations; No 113 flew its last Blenheim sorties on 15 August; and No 42 Squadron finally discarded its Blenheim Vs in September/October 1943. All five squadrons then received Hurricane fighter-bombers.

If proof were needed that 'old soldiers never die', the Blenheim in Burma was a case in point, as recorded by P. G. Bowen, a navigator with No 176 Squadron's detachment of Beaufighters at Imphal in early 1944:
'At the time I was lucky to be flying with a quite famous pilot who in addition to commanding 176 was also senior RAF officer in the Valley, ie Wg Cdr Henry G. Goddard DFC, AFC. On arrival upon the Kangla strip to the north-east of the town on the Ukral Road, Henry spotted a lonely Bristol Bisley (sic) which had been abandoned after the first retreat from Burma and had stood on the airfield unattended for some two years. The aircraft (No BA191 according to my log book) was not alone, in that Henry found that there was a similar machine in a hangar at Imphal Main. He ordered a bemused Chiefy (Flight Sergeant) to get the Kangla aircraft airworthy, using the other one as a "Christmas tree". His "request" was complied with. On the afternoon of 8 May Henry took BA191 for a test. Shortly before dusk the following evening he returned to the Flight to announce that he was going to make a sortie in the "old girl" and instructed it to be armed up with four 250lb bombs. He then told me to get ready and to try to find an air gunner for the turret. For some reason (?) all our aircrew had something else on that evening, and eventually I found a Geordie LAC armourer prepared to risk his neck.'
'The first sortie was short, just down the Tiddim Road to bomb a large "basha" which the Japs were using as an HQ. Later that evening we went off to Kalewa, some 150 miles south on the river, to have a go at the bridge. On 11 May the same weird "team" went off down the road again to bomb a bridge and to strafe Japanese transport.'

Below:
BA576, a Mk V, in India. R. C. B. Ashworth

10
For Valour

Of the 32 airmen awarded a Victoria Cross throughout World War 2 three went to Blenheim pilots, two of these being posthumous honours. By a quirk of fate, each man was awarded the supreme decoration for his selfless courage and dogged devotion to duty in each of the three major geographical theatres of war, ie the Far East, Middle East and Europe, and therefore might well be regarded as individually epitomising the valour of all Blenheim crews in their respective battle zones. By a further chance, each of the three men 'won' his VC in a different mark of Blenheim. Certainly, each unhesitatingly challenged high odds against personal survival in an aircraft obviously outmoded in concept and abilities at the time of his action; a circumstance which applied to almost every Blenheim crew member, no matter when or where he flew on operations.

The first Blenheim VC — in chronological order of action date — was also the first of three Australian-born airmen to be awarded a VC during World War 2, Hughie Idwal Edwards. The son of Welsh emigrants who settled in Fremantle, Western Australia in 1910, Hughie Edwards was born on 1 August 1914 at Fremantle. In 1934 he enlisted as a private in the local garrison artillery, but in July 1935 he transferred to the RAAF and commenced pilot instruction at Point Cook, receiving his 'wings' in June 1936. He next applied for transfer to the RAF, was commissioned in the RAF on 21 August 1936, and posted initially to No 15 Squadron at Abingdon, flying Hind bombers. In March 1937 he was re-posted to No 90 Squadron at Bicester as the squadron adjutant, where he flew Blenheim Is when the unit began receiving these on 19 May that year. In August 1938, however, Edwards' flying career was almost terminated. Flying near the Scottish border, he ran into a storm which froze the Blenheim's ailerons at 7,000ft. At 5,000ft he ordered his crew to bale out but remained at the controls, still hoping the bring the bomber under control and land. Finally, at 700ft he took to his own parachute only to have it caught on the wireless mast. The subsequent crash broke his right leg, severing the main nerve. There followed nine months in hospital, but his leg became permanently paralysed below the

knee, and it was not until April 1940 that Edwards was declared fit for flying duties again.

In February 1941 Edwards joined 139 Squadron at Horsham St Faiths (now Norwich Airport) to fly Blenheim IVs on daylight operations, but on 11 May, with acting rank of Wing Commander, he was appointed to command No 105 Squadron, another Blenheim IV unit, based nearby at Swanton Morley. Losing little time in getting 'operational' again, Edwards, on 15 June, led six of his squadron's Blenheims searching for enemy shipping, and located a small convoy of eight vessels near the Hague. Attacking at less than 50ft above the waves, he selected a 4,000-tonner as his victim and, heading through a hail of cannon and machine gun fire, he released his bombs at mast height and crippled his target. On 1 July Edwards was awarded a DFC for this and previous sorties.

On 4 July Edwards set out on his 36th operational trip — a low level bombing raid on the industrial complex at Bremen — Operation 'Wreckage' — a repeat of a previously unsuccessful attempt against the same target on 30 June. Leading a total force of 15 Blenheims — nine from 105 Squadron and six from 107 Squadron at Great Massingham — Edwards, in Blenheim IV, V6028, 'D' held the bombers in a tight formation up to the target area; then — as the crews had been briefed — the Blenheims were to separate into loose line-abreast

Right:
Air Commodore Sir Hughie Idwal Edwards VC.

and select individual targets. Once each bomber had completed its task it was to be every man for himself on the run-out and return to base. Crossing the North Sea at a mere 50ft above the water the Blenheims crossed into Germany just south of Cuxhaven, then swung southwards to Bremen. The skies were clear with only thin stratas of wispy cloud some 5-7,000ft above them as they made their final approach. Jinking his way through the outer defence ring of tethered barrage balloons and dodging *overhead* telegraph cables, Edwards broke R/T silence to order the rest into the planned 'spread' formation — the object being to get his men across the target as quickly as possible before the flak defences were able to predict accurately the bombers' position. Nevertheless, the flak gunners were already throwing up a veritable curtain of terrifying opposition at the raiders' height. Holding his buffeting Blenheim steady, Edwards ran across the dock area and released his bomb load, then, keeping as low as possible, ran across the heart of Bremen until he reached the outer suburbs. For those 10 minutes or so he was under constant attack by flak, his aircraft being hit repeatedly along the belly of the fuselage, with one shell bursting in the rear cockpit and wounding his gunner, Sgt G. Quinn DFM.

Banking left, Edwards circled Bremen to observe results and to watch the other Blenheims as these roared over the city on a mile-wide frontage. Three of the original 15 had aborted the sortie shortly after take-off, but the remaining 12 led by Edwards pressed home their attack. Two of 105 Squadron's aircraft became flak victims, both crashing in flames, while 107 Squadron also lost two crews to the pulverising ground fire, including its commander Wg Cdr L. V. E. Petley.

All the Blenheims suffered flak damage as they twisted their way over and away from the target, one of them 'retreating' with severed telegraph cables trailing from its wings and tail unit. Edwards having completed his 'recce', headed towards Bremerhaven and Wilhelmshaven. Skirting Heligoland, he then flew out to sea at zero altitude for some 100 miles north of the Frisians before finally turning west for home. Landing back at base just before noon, he was the last survivor to return. His gunner, Quinn, was extracted from his gun turret by Coles crane and whisked away for medical attention, while the ground crew studied the damage to Edwards' Blenheim — much of the port wingtip missing, no port aileron, a cannon shell in the radio rack, telephone wires round the tail wheel and the under-fuselage looking like a colander with its shell holes.

Below:
Bomb aimer's view of Bremen during the raid led by Hughie Edwards on 4 July 1941. *IWM*

Below:
Flt Sgt 'Paddy' Calder,

Right:
Sqn Ldr A. S. K. Scarf VC

Below:
Flt Sgt Cyril Rich, of 62 Squadron, Malaya, 1941.
Mrs K. Hair

Immediate awards to the survivors of 'Wreckage' included four DFMs, a DFC, and a Bar to Sgt Quinn's DFM; while on 22 July came the award of a Victoria Cross to Hughie Edwards for ' ... the highest possible standard of gallantry and determination'.

Edwards' subsequent wartime career was equally distinguished gaining him a DSO in January 1943 and promotion to Group Captain a month later. Remaining in the RAF after the war Hughie Edwards rose to Air Commodore before finally retiring in September 1963 and returning to his native Australia. Further honours followed and included elevation to knighthood in 1974 and appointment as Governor of West Australia. Air Cdre Sir Hughie Edwards VC, KCMG, CB, DSO OBE, DFC died at his Darling Point home in New South Wales on 5 August 1982 — Australia's most decorated airman.

The second Blenheim VC went to a pilot whose action was not brought to the attention of officialdom until four years after the event, Sqn Ldr Arthur Stewart King Scarf. Known to his family as 'John', and to his many Service friends as 'Pongo', Scarf was born in Wimbledon on 14 June 1913, and was educated mainly at Kings College, Wimbledon. Eventually applying to join the RAF in January 1936, he was accepted for pilot training, receiving his ab initio instruction at the AST, Hamble then progressing to No 9 FTS, Thornaby and ultimately

graduating with his 'wings' on 11 October 1936. His first posting was to No 9 Squadron at Scampton to fly lumbering Handley Page Heyford 'cloth bombers', but on 20 March 1937 he was transferred to No 61 Squadron at Hemswell to fly Hawker Hinds. Just four weeks later, on 18 April, however, Scarf was one of several pilots re-posted to Abingdon to form a new unit, No 62 Squadron, initially flying Hinds, which moved base to Cranfield in June 1937. The escalating expansion of the RAF at that period saw 62 Squadron soon being re-equipped with Blenheim Is, the first two examples arriving at Cranfield on 9 February 1938.

In August 1939 Scarf, flying Blenheim I, L1258, JO-B left England with the rest of 62 Squadron bound for Singapore, via India, arriving eventually at Tengah airfield. In February 1941 the unit made a further move of base, this time northwards to Alor Star airfield in the Kedah Province of Malaya, close to the border of (then) neutral Siam. This particular move had resulted from an increasing apprehension among Allied leadership of Japan's ultimate intentions towards Malaya, it being considered highly

Above:
Blenheim I, L1134, PT-F of 62 Squadron taxying out at Tengah, Singapore, February 1941. It was in this machine that Sqn Ldr Scarf 'won' his posthumous VC on 9 December 1941. *IWM*

probable that any Japanese invasion of the Malay Peninsula would be initiated through Siam; hence 62 Squadron was poised as one part of the RAF's firstline defences directly in the path of any such incursion. These fears were realised only too well when, during the early hours of 8 December 1941 (local dateline), Japanese invasion troops beached at Kota Bahru on the east coast. RAF reaction was relatively quick, with five squadrons ordered to carry out a dawn attack on these invaders. No 62 Squadron's crews, unable to find their prime target in the prevailing rainstorms, found and bombed a gaggle of Japanese barges and landing craft just off the coast. By noon on 8 December Siam's army had surrendered to the Japanese, who rapidly occupied airfields at Singora and Patani and flew in large numbers of fighters and bombers. At Alor Star 62 Squadron's Blenheims were completing refuelling and rearming after the dawn sorties when a formation of some 30 Japanese bombers suddenly appeared overhead and bombed the airstrip, wrecking many Blenheims, damaging others and leaving only two in flyable condition. By working nonstop

that day and night 62 Squadron's groundcrews managed to patch up a few of the least damaged Blenheims, and next day these were moved 45 miles south to Butterworth airstrip.

Confirmation of the Japanese occupation of Singora and Patani airfields led to orders for raids on these targets to be made by 62 Squadron at Butterworth and 34 Squadron's Blenheims from Tengah. The first raid was undertaken by six Blenheims of 34 Squadron (three crewed by 60 Squadron personnel) shortly after midday. Though promised the doubtful protection of Brewster Buffaloes, 34 Squadron's crews never saw their 'escort' and bombed alone, losing three Blenheims, the survivors landing at Butterworth. A second attack, comprised of the remaining flyable Blenheims of 62 and 34 Squadrons, was detailed for a 5pm take-off — it never materialised. Bombed up, fully fuelled and ready for take-off, the first Blenheim to go was Blenheim I, L1134, PT-F piloted by Scarf, with Flt Sgt Cyril Rich manning the solitary 0.303in Lewis gun in the dorsal turret, and Flt Sgt Freddie Calder in the navigator's position. Once airborne, Scarf circuited the airstrip to await the rest of his formation, but at that moment a formation of Japanese bombers appeared and proceeded to bomb the earthbound Blenheims, decimating them in their open, unprotected state. Helpless to intervene, Scarf clung to a slender hope that some might still join him in the

PETROL DUMP

SOFT GROUND.

SOFT GROUND.

WIND S

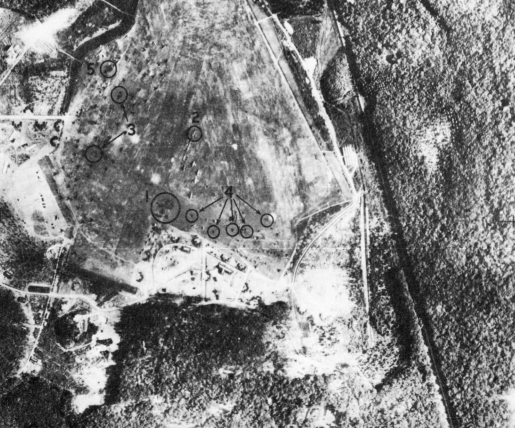

air, but as the enemy bombers fled the scene of devastation, he realised he was alone. Though he would have been fully justified in landing and abandoning the sortie, Scarf's anger and frustration as he watched his friends killed solidified into a stubborn determination to complete his allotted task, and he set course for the Siam border, heading for Singora, some 30 miles deep in Japanese-occupied territory.

Flying low along the plains, Scarf skilfully evaded several attacks by roving Japanese fighters, with Rich effectively preventing these making any close assaults, and as the lone Blenheim crossed the Siam border the fighters withdrew. On nearing Singora, however, fresh fighters closed in. Ignoring these, Scarf made one steady run across the airfield, releasing his bombs, while Cyril Rich fired pointblank into clustered rows of Japanese aircraft parked (in his words) '. . . like a row of taxis'. Completing his bombing run, Scarf turned for the return leg only to run head-on into two formations of Japanese fighters, six in each wave, which bore in for the kill. Jinking his Blenheim almost through the treetops and

huge limestone outcrops, Scarf used every trick and skill be possessed to baffle each succeeding fighter attack, while Cyril Rich used up a total of 17 ammunition drums in crisp bursts in desperate defence. Struck repeatedly by cannon shells and machine gun bullets, the Blenheim became literally riddled.

Scarf, strapped immobile in his unarmoured seat, was soon badly wounded. One burst of fire shattered his left arm (he was left-handed), while other bullets smashed through his seat into his back. As he fell forward over the controls from the impact of his back wounds, Freddie Calder yelled to Rich for assistance. Rich left his turret, passed an arm round Scarf's chest and held him back in his seat while the still-conscious pilot continued to guide his crippled aircraft southwards. The last fighters finally withdrew leaving the bomber to its fate. Only minutes later the wallowing Blenheim arrived over Alor Star airfield and Scarf decided to land there if possible. Next to the airstrip was Alor Star Hospital, in which was Scarf's wife, 'Sally' Lunn, a regular Army Sister in the QAIMNS whom he'd married in April 1941, and who had volunteered for duty at Alor Star wtih the Colonial Nursing Service in order to be near her husband. With Rich still supporting Scarf in his seat, and Calder helping with Scarf's grip on the control column, the Blenheim came in at 300ft, lowering flaps and undercarriage alternately, then retracted its wheels and steadily skimmed across the many mud-banked rice paddy fields, finally ploughing through two feet of water-soaked riceshoots and sliding to a halt about 100 yards from the hospital.

Rich and Calder gently eased Scarf out of his cockpit on to the wing, then, oblivious of their petrol-soaked aircraft, lit up three cigarettes and calmly awaited the many hospital staff running towards them. Transferred to a stretcher and given a shot of morphia, Scarf remained fully conscious as he was quickly taken into the hospital. Doctors, though doubtful of saving Scarf's shattered arm, wanted to operate immediately, but Scarf's serious loss of blood necessitated an immediate blood transfusion. Among the donors was Scarf's wife, Sally, with whom Scarf continued to joke as staff wheeled him into the operating theatre. Then, as Sally left the theatre, Scarf died — due mainly to massive secondary shock and his ultra-weakened condition. In the subsequent chaos and tragedies of the 1941-42 disastrous Malayan campaign most official records were lost or deliberately destroyed; hence, it was not until 1946 that the full details of Scarf's last sortie were brought to the notice of RAF higher authorities. On 21 June 1946 the *London Gazette* announced the posthumous award of a Victoria Cross to Scarf, and his widow received the tiny bronze cross at an investiture on 30 July.

The third Blenheim VC was awarded posthumously too — in this case to a man nurtured

Blenheim V, BA727 at Canrobert airfield, December 1942.

in RAF traditions and code of duty at the Service's own academy, the RAF College, Cranwell. From the date of commencement of the first Cranwell officer-cadet course, 5 February 1920, until September 1939 more than 1,000 cadets had graduated into regular service; and during World War 2, of a total of 931 still serving, 326 lost their lives. Overall, more than 600 decorations for gallantry were awarded to ex-cadets, including three George Crosses, 82 DSOs, 269 DFCs and one Victoria Cross — the latter going to Wg Cdr Hugh Gordon Malcolm. Born at Broughton Ferry, Dundee on 2 May 1917, Malcolm entered Cranwell as a cadet on 9 January 1936, graduated as a pilot in December 1937 and first joined No 26 Squadron at Catterick in the same month, to fly Westland Lysanders in the army co-operation role. While practising for an Empire Air Day on 20 May 1939, however, Malcolm's promising career was almost terminated when he crashed in a Lysander, receiving severe injuries including a fractured skull. Four months later, nevertheless, he was declared fit for flying again and rejoined 26 Squadron on 26 September 1939. The following two years saw Malcolm serve with various units until on 13 April 1942, with the rank of Squadron Leader, he was appointed a Flight commander in No 18 Squadron at Wattisham, to fly Blenheim IV bombers on daylight sorties over Occupied Europe.

Soon after Malcolm took up his latest appointment 18 Squadron became increasingly involved in night 'intruder' sorties in support of main bomber assaults; an example being the night of 30/31 May

1942 when the first Bomber Command '1,000-bomber' raid was flown against Cologne. That night 18 Blenheims of the unit flew intruder sorties against three Luftwaffe base airfields, with Hugh Malcolm leading seven of these against St Trond airfield. By then the increasing obsolescence of the Blenheim IV for pure bombing operations was obvious, and on the night of 17/18 August a Blenheim of 18 Squadron completed the ultimate Blenheim sortie in Bomber Command. A week later 18 Squadron was declared non-operational while it prepared to receive 'new' aircraft and awaited imminent orders to proceed overseas, earmarked as one of several light bomber units for support of a forthcoming invasion of North Africa — Operation 'Torch'. Moving from Wattisham to West Raynham on 24 August, No 18 Squadron began to receive its 'new' aircraft — Blenheim Vs! The squadron also 'received' a new commander when Hugh Malcolm was promoted to Wing Commander in September. In October 1942 the squadron joined three other Blenheim V-equipped units, Nos 13, 114 and 614 Squadrons, to form No 326 Wing, and early in November all moved abroad to Blida, Algeria.

The first operational sortie flown by 18 Squadron in North Africa quickly illustrated the unsuitability of the Blenheim V for its designated role of day-

Above:
Loading a Blenheim V at Canrobert airfield, December 1942.

bomber. On 17 November 1942 Malcolm led his men in an attack on Bizerta airfield in daylight, at low level and without fighter escort. After strafing the target the Blenheims met bad weather and Luftwaffe fighters on the return leg, losing two aircraft in an air collision and two more to the German fighters. Returning to Bizerta on 28 November, Malcolm again led his crews through a fury of flak to bomb the landing ground, then deliberately made several more passes across the target gun-strafing ground installations and parked aircraft. On 4 December 11 Blenheims of 326 Wing were flown to a forward landing strip at Souk-el-Arba for close tactical support bombing sorties in aid of the Allied ground troops in that area. At 09.15hrs that day six Blenheim Vs, led by Malcolm, took off to search for German troop concentrations in the Chougui area and eventually discovered a German airstrip some 10 miles north of Chougui. Bombing and gunning this target, Malcolm led his men back, landing at Canrobert at noon to refuel prior to eventually returning to Souk-el-Arba. Within an hour of landing, however, Malcolm received a message from a forward army battle zone, requesting further immediate air support in the area he had just attacked. It would mean a daylight attack, over a fiercely contested battle zone and without fighter

escort — the latter could not be organised in such a short space of time. Though fully aware of these aspects, Malcolm decided to fly the sortie — his prime duty was to helping the ground troops.

All 11 Blenheim Vs available at Souk-el-Arba — a mixed bag from all three squadrons of 326 Wing — were bombed up and fuelled for the sortie and at 15.15hrs Malcolm led them off in Blenheim V, BA875, 'W' of 18 Squadron, with his crew of two, Plt Offs J. Robb (Nav) and Jimmy Grant DFC (Wop/AG). Behind him one Blenheim burst its tail wheel and slewed off the runway, but the remaining nine got airborne and closed in tight formation — their only defence if they met Luftwaffe fighters. Two fighter sweeps of Spitfires from Souk-el-Arba, and a third from Bone, had left some 10 minutes before the bombers, ostensibly to patrol the Chougui area, but to all intents the Blenheims were on their own. Only 20 minutes after take-off a Blenheim of 614 Squadron (BA825, 'J') developed engine trouble and crashlanded 15 miles east of Souk-el-Arba, though without any crew injuries. Malcolm now had just eight Blenheims behind him — four from 614 Squadron (BA734, BA800, BA869 and BA820), and four from 13 Squadron (BA796, BA769, BA795 and BA862) — and as they neared the forward fighting zone German observers signalled their approach to the nearest Luftwaffe fighters' base, where Gruppen I and II of *Jagdgeschwader 2* were alerted, then despatched to intercept the incoming bombers. Reaching their objective, the Blenheims circled once, then commenced their bombing runs — only to be

Above:
Blenheim Vs on a sortie over North Africa, believed to be 614 Squadron. *IWM*

immediately jumped by a horde of at least 50 Messerschmitt Bf109s. The next five minutes witnessed a massacre of the bombers. Oberleutnant Julius Meimberg later described his view of the action:

'In the afternoon we heard that 12 Bostons* are on their way to Mateur. We sighted these and chased them; the bombers were flying at very low level. All the Bf109s attacked immediately and one Boston was on the ground in flames already before I had a chance of opening fire. I attack one and it starts to

burn at once, losing height and crashing. I then attacked one on the left and, as I am flying in a curve, I can see five already shot down. Several Bf109s at this time are in quite a crowd behind the Yankees (sic). I then shoot down a third which goes down burning and crashes. I can only fire a little at the fourth I attack as all my ammunition is then gone. The battle only lasted five minutes.'

The massive German fighter opposition afterwards claimed a total of 12 bombers destroyed, but three Blenheims survived the first onslaught and crash-landed within Allied lines, four crew members being injured and all three aircraft being wrecked. From the scanty evidence now available Malcolm's Blenheim was one of the last to be shot down, crashing and erupting in flames some 15 miles west of the target. An infantry officer and two other men arrived on the scene minutes later and managed to retrieve James Robb's body, but Malcolm and Grant perished in the flames. Malcolm's courage and his determination to fulfil his duty led to the posthumous award of a Victoria Cross on 27 April 1943.

*Meimberg was unfamiliar with Blenheim aircraft, hence this mistaken identification of type.

11
Canadian
Cousins

The name Bolingbroke was originally applied to a production Blenheim Mk I, K7072, which had been selected to become the prototype Type 149 with a redesigned, extended nose compartment. In its initial configuration it was titled Bolingbroke I and first test-flown on 24 September 1937. With subsequent modification and refinement of the 'long-nose' compartment et al, it was accepted for production in mid-1938 but was retitled Blenheim IV. Licence produc-

tion of the Blenheim IV in Canada was granted to Fairchild Aircraft Ltd of Longueuil, Quebec, and the name Bolingbroke was revived to be applied to this firm's production versions. The first contract awarded to Fairchild was for 18 aircraft for coastal reconnaissance duties by the Canadian Department of National Defence. These were built from Bristol drawings and imported components, and fitted with Mercury VIII engines. As such they were designated Bolingbroke Is and allotted RCAF serials 702-719; the first of the batch, No 702 entering RCAF service

Below:
K7072, which went to Canada on 2 October 1940; the first machine to be titled Bolingbroke.

Bottom:
Bolingbroke I, No 702, the first Canadian-built example which entered RCAF service with No 8 Squadron on 15 November 1939 as YO-A. *BAe*

as YO-A on 15 November 1939 with No 8 Squadron RCAF, and later seeing service with No 119(B) Squadron as DM-A, and No 147 Squadron. Bolingbroke I, No 705 crashed during its test programme, but was then rebuilt and modified with American equipment and instrumentation to become titled Bolingbroke II, while No 717 was delivered in August 1940 fitted with twin Edo floats as Bolingbroke III for evaluation as a floatplane, though it later reverted to landplane configuration. The final production machine of this batch, No 719, was accepted in August 1940 and saw service with the RCAF.

Subsequent production batches, RCAF serials 9001-9201, and 9851-10256, brought the total Fairchild production of all marks of Bolingbroke to 656 aircraft. All were built to 'American' standards, ie directly derived from the Bolingbroke II variant, and were designated Bolingbroke IVs, with first deliveries going to No 8(BR) Squadron RCAF from January 1941. Apart from the Mercury-engined IVs, other versions were fitted with American powerplants. Bolingbroke IVs 9005 and 9010-9023 were fitted with twin 825hp Pratt & Whitney Twin Wasp Junior engines, and were titled IV-W; while No 9074 was

experimentally fitted with two 900hp Wright Cyclones, being designated IV-C accordingly. The final batch, Nos 9851-10256 (plus 51 spare airframes) were built as IVTs — the 'T' signifying a general purpose training version which commenced deliveries to the RCAF in early 1942. Various other 'one-off' experimental trials were made on individual Bolingbroke IVs, including dual-control modified machines, eg 9071 and 9073, and No 9086 which was used to test ski undercarriage gear; while the final production machines (Nos 10200-10256) had Mercury XX* engines installed.

The Bolingbroke was to give relatively long service to the RCAF, with a total of eight squadrons being equipped with the type at varying periods:

Squadron	Dates of use	Squadron codes
8	Dec 1940-Aug 1943	YO
13	Oct 1941-June 1942	AN
115	Aug 1941-Aug 1943	BK, later UV
119	July 1940-June 1942	DM, later GR
121	Aug 1942-May 1944	JY, later EN
122	Aug 1942-Sep 1945	AG
147	July 1942-Mar 1944	SZ
163	Mar 1943-June 1943	Nil

Above and below:
**Two views of Bolingbroke No 717 fitted with Edo floats,
circa August 1940.** *BAe*

Above left:
Twelve of the 14 Bolingbroke IV-Ws (Pratt & Whitney Twin Wasp engines) delivered to the RCAF in mid–1941. *BAe*

Above :
Bolingbroke IV-T, No 10103 at St Hubert, 1943. *BAe*

Left:
Bolingbroke No 9161 in black/yellow striping.
W. T. Larkins

Of these, two became involved in the combined American-Canadian defence campaign to protect the Aleutian Islands and Alaska's western coast. No 115 Squadron, commanded by Sqn Ldr E. M. Reyno, moved to the area (Annette Island, Alaska) in April 1942, and flew its first operational sortie on 13 May when Flt Lt F. B. Curry piloted Bolingbroke IV, 9060, on an anti-submarine patrol. In June 1942 No 8 Squadron, led by its commander Sqn Ldr C. A. Willis, undertook a 1,000-mile flight from RCAF Sea Island north to Yakutat, arriving there on 3 June with 12 Bolingbrokes (later 14). Their presence was part of the American-Canadian force assembled to face Japanese threats to Alaska and the western coasts of Canada and the USA. On arrival one of the first orders to be received by the Bolingbroke squadrons was to paint over the red centres of the upper wing-roundels — ostensibly to avoid confusion in the air with Japanese markings — and, later, to paint a 14in wide blue band around the tail end of the fuselage.

The Aleutians campaign, which was to last until September 1943, was in the main a dull, frustrating period of operations for the Allied aircrews involved. As well as primitive living and operating conditions, and the isolation from civilised amenities, there was the great hazard of raw Nature's highly changeable weather in that area; sudden thick Alaskan fogs from sea to cloud level claimed several lives in mountainside crashes. The Bolingbroke crews spent

most days in states of readiness, with at least two aircraft, armed with 300lb depth charges, taking off on routine anti-submarine and shipping patrols daily. The only recorded encounter with a Japanese submarine came on 7 July 1942, when Flt Sgt P. M. G. Thomas of 115 Squadron bombed the Ro32, then summoned some US Navy ships to the scene who claimed the submarine as sunk. In fact, postwar research in Japanese records show no such loss, and indeed show that Ro32 was still in service in August 1945. Yet another frustration for the Bolingbroke units was the constant lack of spare components for maintenance, nearly all such items being unobtainable from nearby American stores and having to be supplied from faraway Canadian depots. It meant long hours of inventive ingenuity on the part of the long-suffering groundcrews, whose work usually took place in the open air or, at best, under canvas. By the close of 1942, however, Japanese submarines were operating well beyond any Bolingbroke's operational range, and long-range Consolidated B-24 Liberators in RCAF livery were becoming available to replace the type. Accordingly, the Bolingbroke squadrons were withdrawn from the Aleutians zone, No 8 Squadron returning to Sea Island by early March 1943 and 115 Squadron returning to Patricia Bay, British Columbia by late August 1943.

The remaining RCAF Bolingbroke units were, in the main, employed on coastal anti-submarine, convoy escort, photographic or straight training duties; though it is of interest to note that prior to the Aleutians campaign some Bolingbroke I aircraft of 119 Squadron had been 'converted' to fighters by an additional gun pack under the bomb bay position, these being transferred to 115 Squadron in August 1941. Many of these squadrons based in defence of Canada's Atlantic seaboard had as their prime responsibility the protection of Allied merchant convoys, particularly around the selected western terminus and assembly point at Bedford Basin, Halifax. German U-boat activities, which reached their peak from early 1942 to mid-1943, included such daring penetrations as forays into the St Lawrence to seek their shipping prey. For the Boling-

broke crews it meant many operational flying hours 'watching water', with no positive results to show for their dogged routine. No submarines were sunk and only a handful fleetingly sighted, though it is impossible to verify how many U-boat captains (if any) were actually deterred from attacks by the omnipresent RCAF aircraft overhead.

As with so many firstline aircraft of World War 2, the Bolingbroke lingered only briefly on the postwar aviation scene, once its 'useful' life ceased, and today (1983) few remain for present generations to view. Appropriately, one Bolingbroke IVT, No 9892, was purchased as war surplus in 1946, given to Canadian museum authorities in 1963 by Mr George Maude of Fulford, British Columbia, then refurbished in the wartime livery of an 8 Squadron RCAF machine, marked YO-X and displayed at the National Air Museum, Ottawa. Another Bolingbroke, No 10001, has been 'converted' to Blenheim IV status, reserialled as L8756 — the original such serial appearing on a Blenheim IV, XD-E of 139 Squadron, which machine was ultimately struck off Service charge in May 1944 — and is now on display within the RAF Hendon Museum complex. Bolingbroke No 9940, for many years part of the Strathallan Collection in Scotland, was bought at auction in 1981 for £18,000 on behalf of the Royal Scottish Museum. Two more Bolingbrokes resident in the UK are Nos 9896 and 10038, once owned privately by the late O. A. Haydon-Baillie, and now at the former RAF station Duxford. No 9896 is destined for conversion to a 'static display' Blenheim, while No 10038 is being patiently rebuilt to flying condition, and will ultimately emerge marked as V6028, GB-D of 105 Squadron, the aircraft flown by the late Air Cdre Sir Hughie Edwards on the sortie which led to the award of his Victoria Cross. Other Bolingbroke or Blenheim 'relics' exist and, thanks to the enthusiasm and expertise of several groups of private aviation 'archaeologists', may yet emerge as memorials to a 'minor classic' military aircraft.

12
From the
Cockpit

Pilots' views and opinions of the various marks of Blenheim differed widely, though it must be recognised that individual thoughts on the aircraft depended primarily upon the circumstances and operational contexts applicable. To the men who made their first flights in a Blenheim in 1938-39, having been mostly accustomed to biplanes or light single-engined monoplanes, the aircraft appeared something of a monster with its large twin engines, retractable undercarriage, lengthy wing flaps, etc. One such pilot, already well experienced on other aircraft, was H. A. Taylor who, in September 1939 as a member of the Air Transport Auxiliary (ATA) was sent to the RAF's Central Flying School (CFS) at Upavon for a short 'conversion' course on various 'modern' aircraft designs. In his own words:

'After a couple of hours or so on the Harvard advanced trainer and an hour in a Battle light bomber, on which no dual instruction was possible, some of us were led to a Blenheim to see if we could cope with this twin-engined monster.'

'The Blenheim was a small aeroplane by present-day military standards ... but it was a hot affair by the standards of those days and quite a few pilots had been killed through lack of understanding of engine-failure handling techniques. Once mastered, it was a beautiful aeroplane to fly. In the Mark I version, the pilot sat on a kind of dais in a glasshouse; he could see ahead, below and nearly all round him except where the two engines sprouted out of the wing. When, in my turn, I had been shown around the Blenheim's alarmingly complicated control cabin, the CFS instructor airily waved me into the left-hand seat and settled himself down beside me in a seat where the dual-instruction arrangements were, to say the last of it, somewhat primitive. Did the instructor know that I'd never flown anything like this before? He did. "There is nothing to it", he said, and began to go through the

Below:
Blenheim I cockpit, with blind-flying instrument panel fitted, in India, 8 September 1939.
Sqn Ldr L. W. Davies FRGS

engine-starting drill. "I'll do a circuit first and then you can have a try".

'Ten minutes later he had folded his arms in his lap while I sweated my way through the take-off drill with the Blenheim sitting across wind at the leeward end of Upavon's small grass airfield. I had already learned the basic mnemonics by which the CFS instructors taught their pupils to remember the essential actions. For take-off the letters were HTMPFG — which I remembered by muttering "Hot-tempered Member of Parliament flaps his gills" — and for the final approach they were HUMPFG, or just HUMP. Hydraulics, Trimmers (and throttle tighteners), Mixture, Propeller Pitch, Flaps (and fuel cocks) and cooling Gills (or radiator shutters) — these were the essential things on take-off. The "U" in the approach mnemonic stood, importantly enough, for Undercarriage. The Blenheim had a pretty odd control layout. On his right the pilot had three little handled plungers — rather like the things in old-fashioned lavatories — and these were pulled up or pushed down according to requirements. That at the back was the master hydraulic control, providing pressure to the main systems or to the retractable gun turret

Above:
**Blenheim IVF control column and incorporated guns'
firing thumb-button.** *Flight International*

as required; the other two operated the undercarriage
and the flaps respectively. The mixture control,
beside the throttles on the pilot's left, had three positions — automatic weak, rich and, dramatically
enough, take-off override. The two-pitch propellers
were controlled by a couple of fore-and-aft moving
plungers in a panel on the left and *behind* the pilot;
with them (luckily protected by a hinged cover) were
similar plungers to operate the engine cut-outs. The
cooling gills were operated mechanically by hand-
wheel.

'Well, there I was, for better or for worse.
Hydraulics selected, rudder and elevator trim
adjusted, throttles tightened, mixture in override,
pitch checked in fine, flaps up, tanks selected and
gills wound closed and then opened a trifle. I turned
the Blenheim into wind and started, gingerly enough,
to open the throttles. I need not have worried. The
Blenheim went quite straight without any throttle
differential and seconds later I had lifted it off the
ground, retrimmed and pulled up the undercarriage
plunger — losing a length of thumb-skin in the
process. "Hold her down", said the instructor, "and
keep holding her down until you've got engine-failure

safety speed". At an indicated 115mph I pulled the
Blenheim up in a climbing turn and reached behind
me for the propeller-pitch knobs.

'After cruising round for a few brief minutes of
familiarisation the Blenheim was brought into the
circuit and I started to go through the approach drill.
Hydraulics checked; undercarriage plunger pushed
down and green lights flickering on; mixture in override; pitch-knobs hammered into fine, the two
Mercurys screaming in turn as the revolutions
increased; and the flap plunger pushed and pulled
quickly back into neutral as the indicator showed the
correct approach setting. As the boundary fence
came up, with the Blenheim floating along on a whiff
of throttle, the flap plunger was slammed down and
left down. As the big split flaps extended, the aircraft
felt as if it had an arrester wire. But we had plenty
of speed and the throttles could be cut halfway
through the flare-out. The Blenheim settled and
stayed settled and an occasional jab of the thumb on
the brake lever served to keep it straight.' *

If such a favourable impression of the Blenheim I
was understandable from pilots excited about handling 'modern' aircraft of the period, it was not a view
universally shared by later crews who actually flew
the type on operations. The chief criticisms of

*'Test Pilot at War'; Ian Allan, 1970.

Blenheims — all Marks — expressed by operational crews concerned the design's lack of real speed, and its poor defensive armament. Such 'defects' were particularly noticeable in the contexts of Mk IVs and Mk Vs in 1941-42 (or even later in certain war zones). Yet another source of frustration was the limited bomb load capable of being carried — often no better than four 250lb GP bombs — which could have relatively little destructive effect upon targets. In its favour was the Blenheim's acknowledged manoeuvrability — at least, in its Mk I and IV versions; though the same could not be attributed to the Blenheim V, which was described by one veteran Blenheim skipper as ' . . . like driving a consumptive lorry compared with a well-serviced Mk IV'. Certainly, few Blenheim crews denied the structural strength of the design, a feature continually 'blessed' by those who returned from operations again and again in flak-riddled Blenheims to make relatively safe landings.

One ex-Blenheim I bomber pilot summed his feelings by saying:
'On the surface it was pleasant to fly, was very manoeuvrable and had few technical vices. Initial reaction — coming from Hind biplane bomber cockpits — was a feeling akin to a cramped goldfish, with all those window-frames surrounding one up front, but the pilot's view forwards, sideways and down was excellent in relation to take-offs and landings.

One-engine landings could be dicey, but provided one remembered to maintain or increase critical speed limits a simple steady circuit with the good engine on the inside of the turn usually produced a safe arrival. The Blenheim's most evil characteristic — and it appeared to apply to all marks — was the minimal chance for pilot survival should he need to take to his brolly (parachute). I personally knew of three men who were forced to bale out, and each one was chopped up by the propellers'.

Mention of the Blenheim's inadequate defensive armament is a salient aspect in the memories of one ex-Wop/AG, Jim Mansell, who flew Blenheims in 1940:
'The Bristol turret, fitted to the Blenheim IV, was an excellent example of man's inhumanity to man — it seemed that the designer had taken a fiendish delight in making it as uncomfortable and inconvenient as possible. The seat was round and not big enough to accommodate even the smallest backside. It went up and down with the depression and elevation of the gun — yes, *one* gun — a Vickers K gun, gas-operated, the ammo being carried in a tensioned pan placed on top. It was October 1940 before the

121

Blenheims of 101 Squadron were equipped with twin Brownings.'

'The radio was the famous (infamous??) 1082/ 1083 with separate anode and diode coils, and controls for the receiver, and coils for the transmitter. It was located on a shelf aft of the turret, and the operator needed both hands to tune in the receiver. By resting his face against a piece of sorbo rubber thoughtfully provided on the central column of the turret the operator, if he was built like a gorilla, could just reach the controls with his fingertips — he couldn't *see* them. He had to tune by touch — which, considering that he wore three pairs of gloves (silk, wool, leather — in that order) indicates how difficult this was to do. In those days, before IFF (Identification Friend or Foe) came into use, when we returned from ops we had to identify ourselves by sending a W/T message known as MSI (Movement Serial Indicator). To do this meant changing frequency from high to medium, and this meant winding out the trailing aerial. This may sound easy enough but the intense numbing cold was so enervating that it required a real effort of will to accomplish it. Add to this the fact that three coils had to be changed which necessitated six swings of the turret with the operator holding the coils on his lap. And all the time that creeping cold which dulled the senses.

'So-called heated Irvin suits were introduced in October 1940 for us. The only heat provided was for hands and feet in the form of hot wires in gloves and boots. The leads ran along the seams of the suit, ending at waist height in an attachment which was

Above:
The cramped nose compartment of a Blenheim I. *IWM*

plugged into the aircraft electrical system. Myself and another Wop/AG were 'invited' to try out the first two heated suits to be introduced on the squadron. We took off for Duisburg and at 2,000ft I plugged in the suit. Feeling no different from usual I assumed it was u/s (unserviceable). We attacked the target at 10,000ft and, having flown at that altitude throughout the trip, we lost height to get into the Great Massingham circuit. I became suddenly aware of a burning sensation in my hands and feet. I unplugged the suit but not before the backs of my hands and my insteps were blistered. The heat had been on all through the trip, yet I hadn't felt a thing.

'Returning to the subject of that turret; to get the thing into the operating position the cupola had to be raised by winding up on a ratchet. This constituted a hazard in that a crash could dislodge the ratchet and bring the heavy cupola down on the gunner's head, usually breaking his neck. In the early morning of 27 September 1940 we, in Blenheim IV, R3689* were returning from a raid on the harbour at Calais. We were last into the circuit and had to wait our turn. To complicate matters further there was an intruder warning as we finally prepared to land. So, when we finally got the green, we had been hanging around for just under an hour. The wind direction

*Blenheim IV, R3689 later served with 60 Squadron in India in 1942.

Above:
Bomb aimer and his 'tools' in a Mk IV. *IWM*

meantime had changed — but the flare path had not. On the downwind leg I vacated the turret to turn off the oxygen, the bottles being located forward of the top hatch. I was returning to the turret when I felt the flaps go down, so I stood in the well holding the ladder. Next moment all hell broke loose. There was a rending, tearing, grinding crash and I was flung around the fuselage like a rag doll. It seemed to go on for ages but suddenly there was silence apart from the sound of an ominous drip, drip. I found I was still holding the ladder and all in one piece, so I opened the hatch and crawled out on to the fuselage. It was pitch black but I could just make out that both wings had gone. I crawled along the top towards the nose, dreading what I might find there. My skipper, Sgt Bill Tucker, always opened his top hatch a little way before making his approach. As my fingers closed over the edge, the hatch was opened from below. Both Bill and our navigator, Sgt Pat Forder, were unharmed. The nose had concertinaed right back to their feet, as they sat side by side. I went back to look at the turret. The ratchet had broken and the cupola had crashed down, smashing the perspex. Had I been sitting in my usual position on landing, my head would have taken the full impact.

'The Bristol turret was so designed that if the occupant was killed or badly injured in action, there was no way of getting him out. To allow for this situation there was at the bottom of the turret a lever which activated a release valve in the hydraulic system. The weight of the gunner was then sufficient to bring him down far enough to be extricated. It was

called "Dead Man's Lever". The very first time I heard it given this sinister title was by a sergeant armourer lecturing us u/t (untrained) air gunners. I felt then a shiver of apprehension, as I was to feel every other time I heard the name, and was to see it used on more than one occasion in those desperate days of 1940.'

If opinions varied about the Mk I or Mk IV Blenheims, there was virtual unanimity about the Mk V, or so-termed Bisley variant. In a word, 'hopeless'. The additional weight imposed by armour-plating, different turret, bomb load etc merely reduced the Mk V's performance compared to a Mk IV, while manoeuvrability, inevitably, suffered too. As one 18 Squadron pilot opined:
'After the Mk IV, the Bisley (sic) felt like a carthouse after a fairly lively mare. It was sluggish on controls, heavy to manoeuvre, lacked any real urge when necessity arose — such as attempting to get away from pursuing Messerschmitts — and all round proved disappointing, to say the very least. The improved defence, ie twin Brownings in the dorsal turret instead of VGOs, sounded fine, but hardly compensated for all the other deficiencies in speed and agility. Put bluntly, by late 1942 the Mk V was a death trap for its crews when facing any determined German fighter opposition.'

123

Appendices

Consumptions per hour, 62.5% power: Fuel — 55.6gal (253litre);p 417lb (189kg)
Oil — 2.64gal (12litre); 23.80lb (10.80kg)

1 Blenheim Data

BLENHEIM MK I (Manufacturer's figures)

Dimensions

	Ft/In	Metres
Span, main planes	56 4	17.16
Span, tail plane	16 8	5.08
Overall length	39 9	12.12
Height (Rigging position)	15 0	4.572
Height (tail on ground)	9 10	3.00
Max body depth	5 6	1.678
Max body width	4	1.320
Chord (c/plane root)	11 6	3.505
Chord (wingtip)	6 0	1.829
Incidence (main planes)	1deg	
Dihedral, wings	6½deg	
Span, ailerons	8 3	2.512
Max chord, ailerons	2 3	0.686
Span, elevators	16 4	4.977
Root chord, tail plane	3 5	1.041
Wheel track	15 6	4.724
Engine centres	15 6	4.724

Areas

	Sq Ft	Sq Metres
Main planes, inc ailerons	469.00	43.57
Main planes, clear of fuselage	420.00	39.018
Ailerons, inc trim strips	30.6	2.842
Fin	10.4	0.967
Rudder, inc trim flaps	25.65	2.385
Tail plane	40.76	3.791
Elevators, inc trim flaps	29.91	2.782
Wing & centre plane flaps	64.80	5.926

Power Plant: Two Bristol Mercury VIII nine-cylinder, air-cooled, supercharged radials, geared 0.572:1

Airscrews: De Havilland-Hamilton metal three-blade, two-position, hydraulically operated with a diameter of 10ft 6in (3.023m)

Undercarriage: Two single backward retracting Dunlop, 885mm×305mm wheels with Vickers Oleo Pneumatic shock absorbers

Tankage: Fuel — Two 139gal tanks (total, 278gal/ 1,264.4litre)
Oil — Two 8½gal tanks (total, 17gal/77.3litre)

Weights

	Lb	Kg
Powerplant	3,554	1,611
Fuselage	1,111	504
Tail group	268	121.5
Wings	2,476	1,122.5
Disposable	4,621	2,097
Crew of three	600	272*
Empty	7,409	3,360
Loaded	12,030	4,457

* Estimated

Performance (full load)

	Mph	Km/hr
Max speed, sea level	220	354
Max speed, 15,000ft	279	449
Max speed, 10,000ft	265	426
Max speed, 5,000ft	247	397
Cruising (normal)	200	322
Stalling	71	113
Take off in	330yd (305m)	
Landing in	400yd (370m)	
Duration	5hr	
Range	1,000 miles (1,609km)	

Climbs

Initial rate	1,785ft/min (9.1m/sec)
To 5,000ft	2.8min
To 10,000ft	5.5min
To 15,000ft	8.8min
To 20,000ft	13min
Service ceiling	30,000ft (9,840m)

Armament

Bomb load to 1,000lb in fuselage centre-section bays
One 0.303in Browning MG in port wing
One/two 0.303in Vickers Gas-Operated (VGO) 'K' MG in dorsal turret; later, one/two 0.303in Browning MG in dorsal turret
Four 0.303in Browning MG in ventral pack for Mk IF versions only

BLENHEIM MK IV

In overall terms, the standard Blenheim Mk IV was structurally similar to the standard Mk I, with the following differences:
Powerplant: Two Bristol Mercury XV of max 995bhp
Tankage: Two inner wing fuel tanks, each of 140gal
Two outer wing fuel tanks, each of 94gal (long range)
Two main oil tanks, one in each nacelle, each of 11½gal
Two auxiliary oil tanks, each of 2½gal

Dimensions: As per Mk I, except: Overall length 42ft 7in
Height (tail on ground) 12ft 9½in

Weights: All-up — 14,500lb
Max all-up — 15,000lb

Performance

Max speed (11,800ft)	266mph
Stalling	60mph
Service ceiling	22,000ft
Range (1,000lb bomb load)	1,460 miles

Armament: As for Mk I but often with the following additions:
Light Series carriers under each wing for small explosive stores
Under-nose, rear-firing, single 0.303in Browning MG
Rear-firing MG in engine nacelles
One 20mm Hispano cannon in nose in certain Middle East squadrons
NB: Virtually all such 'additions' resulted from local modifications on individual squadrons/units to meet local operational needs.

BLENHEIM V

As for Mk IV generally, with following differences:
Powerplant: Two Bristol Mercury 25 or 30, each 950hp

Dimensions

Span	56ft 1in
Length	43ft 11in
Height	12ft 10in
Wing Area	469sq ft

Weights

Empty	11,000lb
All-up	17,000lb

Performance

Max speed	260mph
Service ceiling	31,000ft
Range (1,000lb bombs)	1,600miles

Armament

Bomb load to 1,000lb
Two 0.303in Browning MG in under-nose, rear-firing 'blister' pack
Two 0.303in Browning MG in Bristol BX dorsal turret

2 Squadrons

The following list refers to RAF squadrons which, at some period, were wholly or partially equipped with some mark(s) of Blenheim. Not all flew the type operationally. The unit code markings indicated were those known to have been allocated officially, but many squadrons, particularly in overseas theatres of operations, did not actually apply these codes to their aircraft.

Squadron	Codes Prewar	Wartime	First equipped
6	—	JV	1941
8	—	HV	May 1939
11	OY	EX	July 1939
13	AN	OO	Aug 1941
14	BF	CX	Sep 1940
15	—	LS	Dec 1939
18	GU	WV	May 1939
20	—	HN	June 1941
21	JP	YH	Aug 1938
23	MS	YP	Dec 1938
25	RX	ZK	Dec 1938
27	—	EG	Jan 1941
29	YB	RO	Dec 1938
30	DP	VT	Jan 1938
34	LB	EG(?)	July 1938
35	—	TL	Nov 1939
39	—	XZ	1939
40	—	BL	Dec 1939
42	—	AW	Feb 1943
44	JW	KM	Dec 1937
45	—	OB	June 1939
52	—	?	Sep 1942
53	TE	PZ	Jan 1939
55	GM	?	May 1939
57	EQ	DX	March 1938
59	PJ	TR	May 1939
60	AD	MU	March 1939
61	LS	QR	Jan 1938
62	JO	PT	Feb 1938
64	XQ	SH	Dec 1938
68	—	WM	Jan 1941
82	OZ	UX	March 1938
84	UR	PY	Feb 1939
86	—	BX	Dec 1940
88	—	RH	July 1941
90	TW	WP	May 1937
92	—	GR	Oct 1939
101	LU	SR	June 1938
104	PO	EP	May 1938
105	—	GB	June 1940
107	BZ	OM	Aug 1938
108	MF	LD	June 1938
110	AY	VE	Dec 1937
113	BT	AD	June 1939
114	FD	RT	March 1937
139	SY	XD	July 1937

	Codes		
Squadron	Prewar	Wartime	First equipped
140	—	ZW	Sep 1941
141	—	TW	Dec 1939
143	—	?	Sep 1941
144	—	PL	Sep 1937
145	—	SO	Oct 1939
162	—	GK	March 1942
173	—	?	1942
203	—	?	May 1940
211	LJ	UQ	May 1939
212	—	?	Feb 1940
218	—	HA	June 1940
219	—	FK	Oct 1939
222	—	ZD	Oct 1939
223	—	AO	1941
226	—	MQ	May 1941
229	—	RE	Nov 1939
233	—	ZS	1939
234	—	AZ	Oct 1939
235	—	LA	Feb 1940
236	—	FA	Oct 1939
242	—	LE	Dec 1939
244	—	?	Feb 1941
245	—	DX	Nov 1939
248	—	WR	Dec 1939
252	—	PN	Dec 1940
254	—	QY	Nov 1939
272	—	XK	Nov 1940
285	—	VG	1941
287	—	KZ	Nov 1941
288	—	RP	Nov 1941
289	—	YE	Nov 1941
404	—	EE	April 1941
406	—	HU	May 1941
407	—	RR	May 1941
415	—	GX	Aug 1941
454	—	—	Nov 1942
489	—	XA(?)	Jan 1942
500	—	MK	April 1941
516	—	?	May 1943
521	—	50(?)	Aug 1942
526	—	MD	June 1943
527	—	WN	June 1943
528	—	?	June 1943
600	MV	BQ	Sep 1938
601	YN	UF	Jan 1939
604	WQ	NG	Aug 1939
608	—	UL	Feb 1941
614	—	LJ	Aug 1942

NB: Query marks indicate uncorroborated documentary evidence of allocation/use. Corrections and/or additional authenticated evidence would be welcomed by the author.

3 UK Production & Serials

B Bristol Aeroplane Co; **A** A. V. Roe, Chedderton; **R** Rootes Securities Ltd

Batch	Manu-facturers	Remarks
Mk I		
K7033-K7182	B	K7033, prototype Mk I; K7072, became prototype IV
L1097-L1546	B	
L4817-L4834	B	
L6594-L6843	A	
L8362-L8407	R	
L8433-L8482	R	
L8500-L8549	R	
L8597-L8632	R	
L8652-L8701	R	
L8714-L8731	R	
Mk IV		
L4835-L4902	B	
L8732-L8761	R	
L8776-L8800	R	
L8827-L8876	R	
L9020-L9044	R	
L9170-L9218	R	Initially built as Mk I, but converted to Mk IV
L9237-L9273	R	Initially built as Mk I, but converted to Mk IV
L9294-L9342	R	
L9375-L9422	R	
L9446-L9482	R	
N3522-N3545	A	
N3551-N3575	A	
N3578-N3604	A	
N3608-N3631	A	
N6140-N6174	B	
N6176-N6220	B	
N6223-N6242	B	
P4825-P4864	B	
P4898-P4927	B	
P6885-P6934	B	
P6950-P6961	B	
R2770-R2799	A	
R3590-R3639	R	
R3660-R3709	R	
R3730-R3779	R	
R3800-R3849	R	
R3870-R3919	R	
T1792-T1832	R	
T1848-T1897	R	
T1921-T1960	R	
T1985-T2004	R	
T2031-T2080	R	
T2112-T2141	R	

Batch	Manufacturers	Remarks	Batch	Manufacturers	Remarks
T2161-T2190	R		**Mk V**		
T2216-T2255	R		AD657	B	Prototype Bisley/V
T2273-T2292	R		AD661	B	Prototype Bisley/V
T2318-T2357	R		AZ861-AZ905	R	
T2381-T2400	R		AZ922-AZ971	R	
T2425-T2444	R		AZ984-AZ999	R	
V5370-V5399	R		BA100-BA172	R	
V5420-V5469	R		BA191-BA215	R	
V5490-V5539	R		BA228-BA262	R	
V5560-V5599	R		BA287-BA336	R	
V5620-V5659	R		BA365-BA409	R	
V5680-V5699	R		BA424-BA458	R	
V5720-V5769	R		BA471-BA505	R	
V5790-V5829	R		BA522-BA546	R	
V5850-V5899	R		BA575-BA624	R	
V5920-V5969	R		BA647-BA691	R	
V5990-V6039	R		BA708-BA757	R	
V6060-V6099	R		BA780-BA829	R	
V6120-V6149	R		BA844-BA888	R	
V6170-V6199	R		BA907-BA951	R	
V6220-V6269	R		BA978-BA999	R	
V6290-V6339	R		BB100-BB102	R	
V6360-V6399	R		BB135-BB184	R	
V6420-V6469	R		DJ702	R	Prototype to Spec B6/40
V6490-V6529	R		DJ707	R	Prototype to Spec B6/40
Z5721-Z5770	A		EH310-EH355	R	
Z5794-Z5818	A		EH371-EH420	R	
Z5860-Z5909	A		EH438-EH474	R	
Z5947-Z5991	A		EH491-EH517	R	
Z6021-Z6050	A				
Z6070-Z6104	A				
Z6144-Z6193	A				
Z6239-Z6283	A				
Z6333-Z6382	A				
Z6416-Z6455	A				
Z7271-Z7320	R				
Z7340-Z7374	R				
Z7406-Z7455	R				
Z7483-Z7522	R				
Z7577-Z7569	R				
Z7610-Z7654	R				
Z7678-Z7712	R				
Z7754-Z7803	R				
Z7841-Z7860	R				
Z7879-Z7928	R				
Z7958-Z7992	R				
Z9533-Z9552	A				
Z9572-Z9621	A				
Z9647-Z9681	A				
Z9706-Z9755	A				
Z9792-Z9836	A				
AE449-AE453	A				

Notes:

1 Serial AX683 applied to ex-L1431 (Mk I) on return to RAF from SAAF.

2 Cancelled production orders not included on listings.

3 Serials quoted in numerical/alphabetical sequence for ease of reference; not in contract dates' order.

4 Non-UK Production & Serials

Finland

BL146-BL190 Valtion Lentokonetehdas, Tampere
BL196-BL205 (Five more not completed)

Yugoslavia

16 Mk Is completed, plus 24 more destroyed before completion. All built at Ikarus A.D., Zemun.

Canada

All Bolingbrokes by Fairchild Aircraft Ltd, Longueuil (RCAF serials)

Mk I:	702-719
Mk IV:	9001-9004
	9006-9009
	9024-9073
	9075-9201
Mk IVW:	9005
	9010-9023
Mk IVC:	9074
Mk IVT:	9851-10256 (plus 51 spare airframes)

Select Bibliography

C. Barnes; *Bristol aircraft since 1910;* Putnam, 1970 (2nd Ed).

Bristol Blenheim Bomber; Bristol Aeroplane Co, 1936.

'Up in a Blenheim'; *Flight,* 24 June 1937.

'Blenheim'; *Aeronautics,* February 1940.

'The Blenheim Family'; *Aeroplane Spotter,* 26 August 1943.

'Bristol Aircraft'; *Flight,* 16 February 1950.

The Book of Bristol Aircraft; Harborough, 1946.

P. J. R. Moyes; *Bristol Blenheim I;* Profile No 93.

J. D. Oughton; *Bristol Blenheim IV;* Profile No 218

Camouflage & Markings No 7; Ducimus Books.

O. Thetford; *Aircraft of the RAF since 1918;* Putnam, 1976 (6th Ed).

J. Goulding; *RAF bombers of WW2;* Hylton Lacy, 1968.

Moyes/Goulding; *RAF Bomber Command, 1936-40;* Ian Allan, 1975.

W. Green; *Famous Bombers of Second World War;* Macdonald, 1960.

P. J. R. Moyes; *Bomber Squadrons of the RAF;* Macdonald, 1964.

J. Rawlings; *Fighter Squadrons of the RAF;* Macdonald, 1969.

J. Rawlings: *Coastal & Support Squadrons of the RAF;* Jane's, 1982.

Kostenuk/Griffin; *RCAF Squadrons & Aircraft;* Stevens, 1977.

J. Halley; *RAF Unit Histories,* 2 Vols; Air Britain, 1969/73.

L. Hunt; *Twenty-One Squadron;* Garnstone Press, 1972.

M. J. F Bowyer; *No 2 Group;* Faber, 1974.

N. J. Roberson; *History of XV Squadron;* Private, 1975.

C. Bowyer; *The Flying Elephants — 27 Squadron;* Macdonald, 1972.

A. N. White; *44 Squadron on operations;* Private, 1977.

D. Warne/A. J. Young; *Sixty Squadron;* 1967.

R. Alexander; *Special Operations — 101 Squadron;* Private, 1979.

D. Ransom; *Battle Axe — 105 Squadron;* Air Britain 1967

Ed. B. Northway; *History of 107 Squadron;* Private, 1964.

E. D. Bell; *110 Squadron History;* Air Britain, 1972.

P. Lambermont; *Lorraine Squadron;* Cassell, 1956.

R. J. Brooks; *Kent's Own — 500 Squadron;* Meresborough, 1982.

T. Moulson; *The Flying Sword — 601 Squadron;* Macdonald, 1964.

T. Wisdom; *Wings over Olympus;* G. Allen, 1942.

Rawnsley/Wright; *Night Fighter;* Chatto & Windus, 1953.

R. Chisholm; *Cover of Darkness;* Chatto & Windus, 1953.

H. A. Taylor, *Test Pilot at War;* Ian Allan, 1970.

J. A. Brown; *A Gathering of Eagles;* Purnell S. A., 1970.

Richards/Saunders; *Royal Air Force, 1939-45,* 3 Vols; HMSO, 1953-54.

A. J. Brookes; *Photo-Reconnaissance;* Ian Allan, 1975.